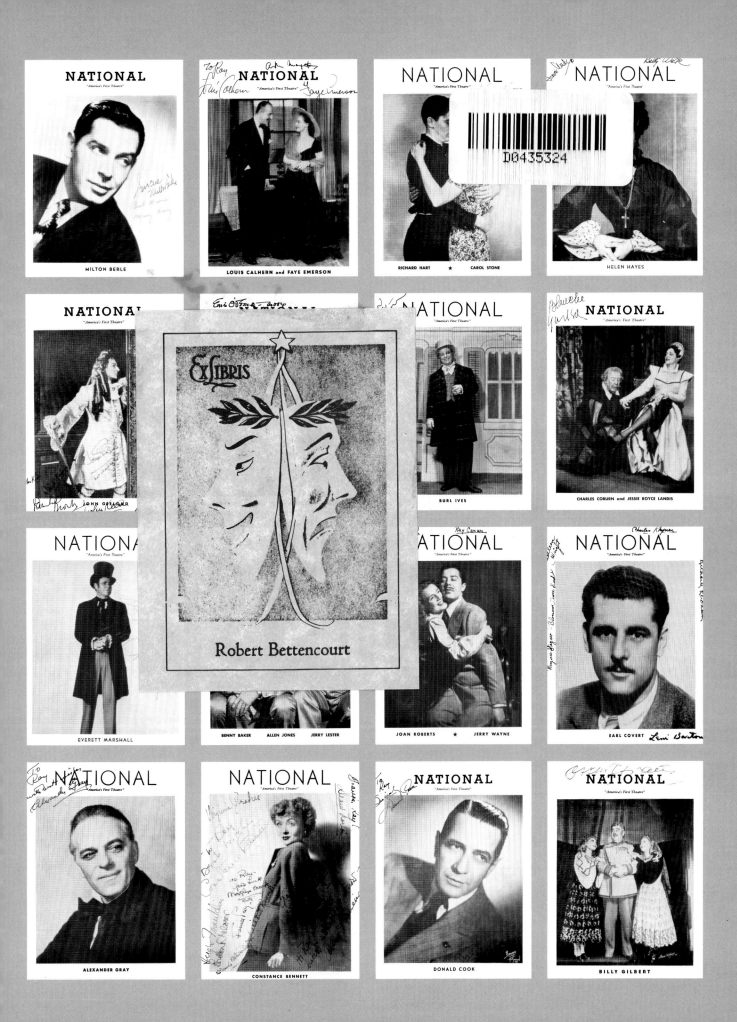

Stage for a Nation

Stage for a Nation

THE NATIONAL THEATRE ★ 150 YEARS

Douglas Bennett Lee

Roger L. Meersman
University of Maryland

Donn B. Murphy
Georgetown University

Foreword by Harry Teter, Jr.

With a Preface by Helen Hayes

UNIVERSITY PRESS OF AMERICA
Lanham ★ New York ★ London

University Press of America, Inc., based in Lanham, Maryland, publishes a wide variety of books about theatre and drama, including all American Theatre Association books and directories. We are pleased to publish this book to celebrate the 150th anniversary of the National Theatre.

4720 Boston Way
Lanham, MD 20706

3 Henrietta Street
London WC2E 8LU England

Co-published by arrangement with the
National Theatre Corporation.

Library of Congress Cataloging-in-Publication Data
    Lee, Douglas Bennett.
    Stage for a nation.

    1. National Theatre (Washington, D.C.) 2. Washington (D.C.)—Buildings, structures, etc.
3. Theater—Washington (D.C.)—History. I. Meersman, Roger L. II. Murphy, Donn B. III. Title.
PN2277.W22N384 1985   792'.09753   85-22761
ISBN 0-8191-5021-5 (alk. paper)

Special photographs by Joseph H. Bailey
Picture editing by Bonnie S. Lawrence
Design by Anne Masters
Research assistance by Abigail Tipton

FOREWORD

As I escorted Miss Helen Hayes to her seat the night of the 1984 reopening of the National Theatre, she paused halfway down the aisle, looked about and exclaimed, "Oh what a wonderful theatre—it is truly a Washington institution." Her joy at seeing the theatre more resplendent than ever, reopening after its seventh major renovation in 150 years, was echoed in the hearts of the audience that evening. All of us were proud that the theatre we have depended on to bring Broadway to the Nation's capital was healthy and doing what it has been doing since it opened December 7, 1835: entertaining its patrons with the finest theatrical productions of the day.

It is an institution, as Miss Hayes said. For a century and a half the National has been one of America's preeminent touring houses. It is an established part of the cultural life of Washington and is its oldest arts institution. In recent years the theatre has been owned by the nonprofit National Theatre Corporation. In 1979 the National entered into a management agreement with The Shubert Organization, the premier theatrical producer and theatre operator in this country, to insure continuous high-quality presentations for the National. Producing attractions of high quality requires a delicate balance of nurturing the artistic talents available and knowing what product the theatre marketplace will accept. Today there are fewer touring shows and they are increasingly more expensive to present. In years past dozens of shows toured each year. Comedies and dramas would play one or two weeks and move on. Musicals would stay a week or two longer. Today longer engagements are necessary to recoup the costs. Shows must be able to stay from several weeks to several months. The competition is keen. The resources of The Shubert Organization have made it possible for the National to have successful long-run engagements and thus be able to bring superior theatrical productions to Washington.

The architecture of the National reflects an era when theatre auditoriums were designed so that actors and audience were drawn together by the resonance of the natural voice and subtle movements of the performers. In this house words can be heard equally as well in the last row of the balcony as in the sixth row center orchestra. On the National's stage, actors can sense the audience's reactions because the interior design brings the audience close to the performers. With its recent remodeling, the theatre combines the elegance of its origins with the comforts and technologies of modern day.

The history of the American theatre has been reflected at the National. Every great star, playwright, composer, director, and producer has brought his or her talent to the National's stage. If the walls of this theatre could talk, what stories they could tell! The legendary figures of show business have all been here.

And so it will continue for the years to come. Audiences will continue to experience the excitement and wonder of theatre at the National. Excitement that begins from the moment the lights dim and the orchestra strikes the first note of the overture to a musical, or the curtain rises to the opening line of a play, and that lasts long after the star takes the final curtain call. This is theatre. This is what the National has been doing successfully for 150 years and what it will continue to do for at least the next 150 years.

The National has always faced Pennsylvania Avenue, the Avenue of the Presidents. Every chief executive since Andrew Jackson has found moments to escape the pressures of their duties and relax at the National. History itself has paraded past the National's doors, often in the form of protest marches in quest of jobs, equality, civil rights, and peace. These concerns and others are reflected also on the stage of the National. The major events of our Nation's history have reverberated on this stage.

The National Theatre greatly appreciates the generous support of the Gould Foundation in producing *Stage for a Nation*. Special recognition is also given to the National Theatre Board of Directors, The Shubert Organization, the employees of the National Theatre, the artists onstage, and those "behind the scenes"— company managers, stage managers, designers, carpenters, wardrobe persons, lighting technicians, stagehands, ushers, box office personnel, sales and press persons, theatre owners and theatre managers—all play a vital part in the theatre's success. Their dedication and devotion to the theatre and to the National keep its lights ablaze.

Harry Teter, Jr.
General Manager, National Theatre

My Dear National Theatre:

From your topmost balcony I saw my very first play. What a wondrous afternoon as I sat there with my mother, mesmerized by the magic of theatre. My heart took flight, and I guess it has not come down to earth yet. When the curtain fell, I refused to leave—and I had to be dragged away. Thus began a lifelong love affair with the theatre.

I have returned many times to perform on your stage, and now I am deeply honored by the naming of the Helen Hayes Gallery in the Theatre. And I am delighted that the Helen Hayes Awards, inaugurated at the National, will recognize distinguished theatrical achievements in Washington.

Now I salute you, my dear friend, on your 150th year! What a pleasure you have given to me and to countless audiences: the magic that begins when the lights dim, the curtain rises, and we are transported from a care-burdened world to one where the imagination and the creative muses lift our spirits high.

Happy Birthday, dearest National, you have only just begun!

Fondly,

Helen Hayes

America's official portrait of Helen Hayes, on loan from the National Portrait Gallery, hangs in the National Theatre.

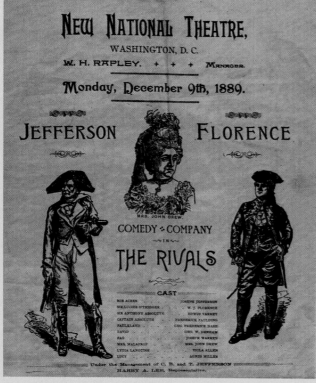

An artist's re-creation of the first National Theatre is based on 1835 newspaper descriptions and the architecture of playhouses in other American cities of the time.

Swedish songstress Jenny Lind arrived for her grand tour of America in 1850. Two of Washington's leading businessmen rebuilt the National—burned in 1845—to accommodate two concerts by Lind for the nation's foremost statesmen and their ladies.

Two great theatrical dynasties, the Jeffersons and the Drew-Barrymores, were represented at a National performance of one of the most popular plays of the late 19th century.

The theatre's most recent restoration, completed in 1984 under the supervision of Broadway designer Oliver Smith, uncovered long-painted-over classical medallions which were repaired and regilded. New painted plasterwork echoes the classical motif in arches above the boxes.

Evenings at the National in its early years invariably featured more than one entertainment. The National's first manager, Thomas Ward, played the male lead opposite visiting star Josephine Clifton in 1837 on a bill that included the popular song "Home Sweet Home."

The great gold eagle atop the proscenium has been adopted as the theatre's official symbol.

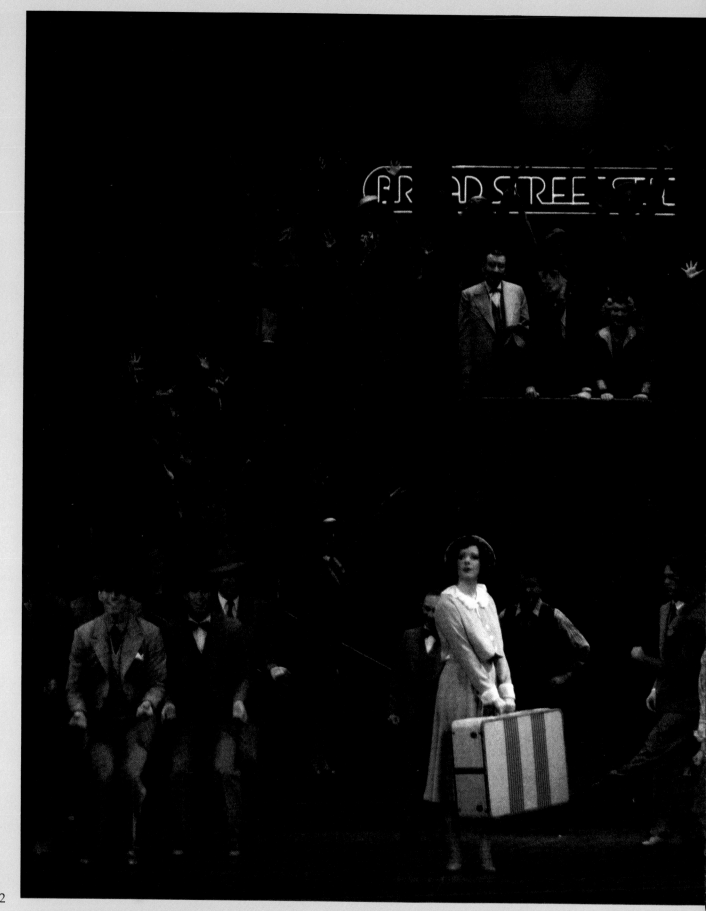

President and Mrs. Reagan came over from the White House to celebrate the National's 1984 reopening. After a rousing performance of 42nd Street, the First Couple joined the cast onstage, where the President greeted the opening night crowd and saluted the National's distinguished history and long survival.

ACT I:

Antebellum Evenings

A NIGHT AT THE NATIONAL

*T*he Indian chiefs in their robes and feather bonnets sat on the left of the theatre and stared in fascination at the dancer dressed as a mountain sylph. Scattered through the larger crowd of Washington's fashionable theatre-goers were more Indians, wearing U.S. military coats with epaulettes, hats with silver bands, leggings, and blankets, gifts given them that day by the "Great White Father," President Martin Van Buren.

They were leaders of the Sioux, Iowas, Sacs, and Foxes from beyond the Great Lakes, come to Washington to make treaties with the nation that was pushing relentlessly into their lands. For all but one it was their first trip to a large settlement, as Washington of the time is best described. Part town, part country, it was a capital still early in its making, where marble edifices rose beside unpaved, unlighted streets that trailed away beyond the last building into uncut woodlands. The daily *National Intelligencer* had observed the Indians on the muddy main streets around Pennsylvania Avenue, reporting them to be "fierce-looking, stout, and able-bodied men" who carried with them their bows and arrows, tomahawks and pikes. The paper had wondered rather nervously if they should be allowed to

French dancer and pantomimist Celine Celeste was a hit of the first National's opening season. She continued to appear before National audiences over the years, flourishing in melodramatic roles such as Miami.

15

Briefly a star in the 1830s, Annette Nelson added war bonnets and wolfskin robes to her Mountain Sylph costume after Indian admirers presented her with them at the National.

wander the capital "armed cap-a-pie, *without their attendants.*" Now, by invitation of the National Theatre's management, they sat in a body in the front rows of Washington's only full-time playhouse, charmed by Miss Annette Nelson in a "Grand Melo-Dramatic Spectacle" entitled *The Mountain Sylph,* and they were about to show their appreciation in a style never again witnessed on the National's stage or any other since that Saturday night in September, 1837.

A "literary gentleman" who wrote an eyewitness account for the *Intelligencer* noticed the ladies of Washington "looking with strange interest on these sons of the forest." Manager Thomas Ward, veteran of the London and Philadelphia stages, would not have found the interest strange at all—with a showman's instinct he had invited the best draw in town into his audience, knowing full well that a spectacle in the seats was worth at least as much for business as one onstage.

Just five years before, Sacs and Foxes had been fighting and fleeing the Illinois militia (among them young Abraham Lincoln) in the frontier conflict known as Blackhawk's War. Blackhawk himself, no longer at war with the United States, was due to arrive in Washington on the morning after Miss Nelson's performance, and

would make a striking entrance to the capital amid a tom-tom beating retinue. So tonight the curiosity of Washington was fixed on Mr. Ward's guests, who were as delighted with Miss Nelson as the ladies in the boxes were fascinated by them.

The Indians had cheered and clapped when the "agile and fairy figure of the Mountain Sylph" entered from on high in a mountaintop setting "and her feet touched lightly the stage. As she moved from place to place, appearing and vanishing with a rapidity that reminded them of the fleetness of the deer in their native hunting grounds, their interest became more intense."

Suddenly that interest translated into action as a young chief of the Yankton Sioux, Pa-la-ne-a-pa-pi, "the Man Struck by Arikara," leapt from his seat and flung his eagle-feather war bonnet onto the stage, praising the dancer in words and "the most expressive looks of approbation."

It was a headdress, we are told, "which he had often worn in bloody conflict with the enemies of his people." Miss Nelson accepted it with aplomb and added it to her costume, a winged affair otherwise notable chiefly for its mid-thigh and daringly decollete brevity.

Not to be outdone, an aged Sac chief named Po-ko-na, "the Plume," whose friendship with the U.S. reached back through the War of 1812, stood and offered a headdress of his own. Next came a leading brave of the Yanktons named To-ka-ca, "the Man That Inflicted the First Wound," with a magnificent robe of white wolfskins "worn only at the most imposing ceremonies of his tribe." Yanktons clinched the honors when second chief Ha-su-za, "the Forked Horn," and "a young brave of rank" named Mou-ka-ush-ka, "the Trembling Earth," presented Miss Nelson with richly ornamented buffalo robes.

"The Trembling Earth," at least, had noticed the attention from the boxes as well as Miss Nelson's charms, for he dedicated his gift "to the beauty of Washington." Miss Nelson replied "with graceful ease," regretting that she could not speak their languages, but thanking them and calling them friends and brethren. "Then, advancing to the box, she presented to each a beautiful ostrich plume, which they immediately placed upon their headdresses." So coifed, the Indians returned to watching and Miss Nelson to her dance. At the play's end, in a flight of inspiration that outsoared even her aerial entrance, the actress fanned the eagle-feather war bonnet across her brow with "a most magical effect."

"It would be vain," the correspondent felt, "to attempt to convey to those who were not present an idea of the impression created by such an unwonted and unexpected exhibition of interest and admiration by these untutored men." Yet the scene is not so hard to picture:

It would have been hazy, just in the slightest, with

soot from the whale-oil lamps and dust. The amphitheater-like main floor loomed cavernous in the dimmed house lights. The theatre was high-domed, with a vault of sky blue adorned with allegorical figures—Power and Wisdom, for example, repelling Tyranny and Superstition. More paintings decorated the boxes and the proscenium arch that framed the stage. Three tiers of boxes rose, the first on a level with the main floor's parquet seating nearest the stage. On the third level and farthest back was the gallery, an open area of bench seating with sections for both whites and blacks.

There would have been a tang of tobacco juice, sweat, rosin, and the waft of burning sperm-whale oil mingling with scents of perfume and powder. Fans rustled in the boxes, while from the gallery came laughter and catcalls. Here and there among the seats were stoves, probably unlit in the lingering warmth of a Washington September. Quite likely a mosquito or two sampled the parquet crowd of government leaders, professionals, merchants, businessmen, shippers, officers, office-holders, and office-seekers.

In the white gallery sat the "gallery gods," as they were known—noisy, opinionated, cheerfully rude 25-cent patrons who could make a performer's evening into a triumph or a fiasco, depending on their mood, or drive a pompous target in the dollar seats below out of the theatre with an apple-core barrage.

Nearby in the "gallery for people of color" sat slaves and free blacks, although the crowd there would have thinned considerably just before ten o'clock when a curfew went into effect for blacks on the streets without approved passes. Those who stayed were most likely slaves who may have arrived at the theatre in the afternoon to save seats for their masters' and mistresses'

The city's first thoroughfare, Pennsylvania Avenue was little more than a cart track when Blodgett's Hotel, at right, housed Washington's earliest theatrical production in 1800. The President's Mansion stands farther down the "Avenue."

more timely arrival, and would accompany them home after watching the evening's entertainment from the third-tier benches.

A few among them must have been the property of avid theatre-goers, and attended the National as often as their owners did. If so, then some of the house's most frequent patrons must have been found high and in the back, silent witnesses to the gaudy cavalcade that marched across the National's stage on a thousand and more antebellum evenings.

In front sat the Indians, ostrich plumes catching the stage lights. Tribal leaders were by no means infrequent visitors to Washington in the decades before the Civil War. They stayed in the city's best hotels and had virtual freedom of the town, and were received by government officials with the honors due representatives of foreign states. A favorite hostelry among these visitors was the Indian Queen (later called Brown's), where a multihued portrait of Pocohantas hung over the entrance a few blocks down Pennyslvania Avenue from the theatre.

The Avenue, with the only sidewalk in the half-built city and most of its stores, hotels, and saloons ranged along its northern side, was the scene of virtually all evening life to be found outside the private salons of Washington's most entrenched society around Lafayette Square. A nightly promenade along the north side (the southern face ran more to gambling spots and houses of ill repute) featured characters from all parts of the country, just as Washington itself reflected the nation with Eastern polish, Southern grace, and more than a touch of frontier rawness.

But rarely even on the Avenue were its disparate parts drawn together into a tableau such as the National presented that night: the leading lights of Washington, gentlemen and ladies, entranced by the "untutored" men from the frontier, who sat proudly wearing feathers from Africa given them by an actress who had emigrated from England, while from far above,

The artistic patron of the National Theatre's founding and early years, Philadelphia's Chestnut Street Theatre was the pride of that city and, in its heyday, America's premiere playhouse.

young white rowdies, black freedmen, and slaves looked on.

It is a scene as thoroughly national as any the theatre's founders could have envisioned at the meeting in 1835 when they voted unanimously in favor of that ambitious name for their new enterprise.

BEGINNINGS

Theatre had been a part of Washington's life almost from the city's birth; inevitably, perhaps, in a city so full of characters, with such a sense for the dramatic and fondness for nightlife. Straddling both Virginia and Maryland, Washington while still a village was heir to the styles and attitudes of the Tidewater aristocrats who had nurtured the earliest English-speaking theatre performed on this side of the Atlantic.

In 1665, in Accomac County on the James River's eastern shore, the author and actors of the first dramatic performance of the colonies were hauled before a magistrate for a production entitled *Ye Bare and Ye Cubb*. Although they were found "not guilty of fault" after re-enacting their play before the judge, the reception was typical of prejudices against acting and

actors that made performing in colonial times a rough and rocky road. Virginia and Maryland were the only colonies without laws against presenting plays.

In 1716 in Williamsburg, capital of colonial Virginia, a theatre opened for performances produced by a merchant and his two indentured servants who had acted and taught dancing and elocution in England. The building soon fell into disuse, and later became the town hall, but it is thought to be the first structure raised specifically for theatrical purposes in English-speaking North America—America's first theatre.

Puritans in Boston, Dutch burghers in New York, and Quakers and Presbyterians in Philadelphia objected to theatre on religious grounds and from belief that it promoted idleness and love of luxury. Rice and indigo planters in Charleston, however, shared the aristocratic backgrounds that disposed their tobacco-planting brethren of the Tidewater toward receiving theatre with pleasure. Charleston's New Theatre on Dock Street opened in 1736. It remained active for only a year, and the site was not used for entertainments again until 1937, when a re-creation of the original playhouse was built. But Charlestonians and their counterparts in Maryland and Virginia were the first to wel-

T.D. Rice introduced blackface minstrelsy to the American theatre in 1828 with the song "Jump, Jim Crow." He was a popular figure at the National's predecessor, the Washington Theatre.

MR THOS. D. RICE.
(of the Theatres Royal,)
THE
JIM CROW.

Thos. D. Rice

International financier W.W. Corcoran, one of Washington's leading philanthropists, was among the prominent citizens who founded the National.

come the visits and ventures that launched theatre on the English-speaking mainland.

New York, too, had theatres in the 1730s, but almost nothing is known of them. The first American acting troupe remembered today, that of Murray and Kean, converted a warehouse in Philadelphia into that city's first theatre in 1749. They went on to reopen the Nassau Street in New York (built in 1732) and to perform in Williamsburg, Annapolis, and other towns in the region.

A turning point in theatre's establishment on these shores came with the arrival, in Virginia in 1752, of a ship called the *Charming Sally*, bearing the first professional British troupe to visit the New World.

Most of its members were third-rate London actors, and their leader, William Hallam, was a bankrupt whose theatre had been closed by debts. But they brought with them high spirits and a zeal for the American adventure that won them success in Williamsburg and Charleston and, despite strong church opposition, in New York and Philadelphia, too.

NEW THEATRE, WASHINGTON.
SEALED proposals for the erection of a new Theatre in Washington City, will be received until the 8th of September, the work to be completed and ready for opening on the 1st day of January, 1835.

General description of the work.

To be located on the open space included between F. street on the north, Pennsylvania Avenue on the south, and 13th street on the east.

Dimensions of the lot.

Front on 13th street, 76 feet 6 inches in length.
Avenue, 150 feet.
Rear 50 feet.
F. street 74 by 79—153.

The principal front, on 13th street, to be arranged according to the Roman Doric style of architecture, consisting of a basement 8 feet 6 inches in height, and 40½ feet in length, with steps all around; 4 Roman Doric columns, with entablature and balustrade; the intercolumniation to be such that the entrance doors to the building shall be in their openings respectively 5½, 6½, and 5½ feet. The lower diameter of the shaft to equal 3 feet 9 inches, and the height of the column 29½ feet, (including plinth and abacus,) to be built of brick and stuccoed, having cast iron capitals and bases. The entablature to be of wood work.

The outer walls of the building to be of the length given above with the general height of 49 feet 6 inches, and to be of the following thicknesses:

From the foundation (which average 3 feet 6 inches below the pavement at the southeast corner of the lot) to the height of 12 feet above, to be 3½ brick thick, to be continued throughout the entire round of the building, (with the exception of the ground beneath the stage, which will be excavated, if possible, to the depth of 8 feet.) From this height (12 feet) the walls will be carried up to the distance of 14½ feet, 3 bricks thick, thence to the eaves of the building, i. e. 23 feet, 2½ bricks.

A wall of the form of a segment of a circle will divide the entrance hall from the box lobbies, to be carried from the foundations to the trussing of the roof, 2 bricks thick. A similar wall will be introduced in rear of the boxes, in thickness 1½ bricks.

Other walls will be introduced into the building at several points, to act as buttresses and partitions to green and dressing rooms.

The Stage will average 68 by 60 feet, to be supported by timbering sufficiently strong to sustain the pressure arising from the introduction of horses if necessary.

The parquette, or pit, to be arranged in such a manner as to admit of being entirely removed, so that the building may be used as an amphitheatre.

The building will require 18 doors, 6 feet by 10½ feet, and the same number of windows, 6 feet by 9½; with such other openings as may be necessary.

The whole interior of the auditory, boxes, galleries, parquette, &c. to consist of workmanship similar to that used in the generality of buildings of this nature in this country; there will be 3 tiers of seats, to be supported by cast iron columns, of which 48 will be necessary.

The plan and elevation may be seen at the present theatre in this city, at any time. Further information can be obtained by an application to Mr. Jefferson, Manager, at his residence.

The first sign of the theatre's imminent arrival appeared in the National Intelligencer *in August, 1834, although the location and dimensions were later changed.*

Joseph Jefferson II never achieved the fame of his father—a popular comedian—or his son—one of the nation's favorite actors—but was active in Philadelphia and Washington theatres and performed in the National's opening show on December 7, 1835.

Headed by David Douglass after Hallam's death, the American Company, as it came to be called, provided the colonies with virtually their only pre-Revolutionary professional theatre. The troupe built playhouses in Williamsburg, New York, Philadelphia, Annapolis, Newport, and Charleston, and appeared in Richmond and Baltimore as well. To avoid religious wrath, shows were often billed as lectures, moral dialogues, or "pantomimical farces." In a famous instance in prim Newport, Douglass advertised a performance of *Othello* as "a series of moral Dialogues in five parts Depicting the evil effects of Jealousy and other Bad Passions and Proving that Happiness can only Spring from the Pursuit of Virtue."

Soon after the Revolution began, the Continental Congress banned theatre and all other public amusements for the duration of the war. Motivated as well by growing anti-British feelings, Douglass retired to Jamaica, and until war's end theatre was seen only in cities occupied by Redcoats and in George Washington's Bluecoat army encampments—notably at Valley Forge.

As soon as was politic, Douglass and company returned to rekindle activity. As demand for entertainment grew rapidly with the size and prosperity of the fledgling nation, groups like one led by Thomas Wig-

Junius Brutus Booth's power lay in the passion he brought to tragedy roles such as Richard III, his premiere Washington part. Booth's engagements at the young National Theatre did much to help it become established as a playhouse of the first rank.

nell split off to found new theatres. By 1800, three distinct theatrical circuits had developed. In the north the American Company—now called the Old American Company—played New York, Boston, and smaller towns. From Charleston another troupe visited North Carolina and Richmond. In the center Wignell's Philadelphia Company reigned supreme, also playing in theatres that Wignell and partner Alexander Reinagle owned in Baltimore and Annapolis. Washington was a natural addition to the center circuit.

Traveling players had appeared in Georgetown and Alexandria in the 1700s, but Washington's first stage performance occurred in August, 1800, pre-dating Congress's arrival in the city by three months. Wignell's Philadelphia Company opened in a white elephant of a building called Blodgett's Hotel on Pennsylvania Avenue, which had been cut through cornfields on the banks of Tiber Creek only four years before.

The Avenue was little more than an elder-bush thicket, while the broad expanse of Tiber Creek covered much of the present-day Mall. The stream frequently spilled over its banks and coursed through the streets, leaving catfish flopping in mud puddles. Before the

first performance was held, just such a flood destroyed the visiting troupe's scenery and stage props brought from Philadelphia. The opening was delayed, and when *Venice Preserved* finally inaugurated the new capital's premiere season, it was performed on a hastily improvised stage set.

The Philadelphia players, most of whom were London-trained emigres, had left their adopted nation's most sophisticated city for one that was mostly woods, and their reaction is reflected in lines from a prologue (written by a local man) read aloud before the first performance:

> *The floods of late, which drowned you many a horse,*
> *Have caused to us a much severer loss—*
> *Our groves, our temples gone beyond repair,*
> *Our gorgeous palaces it did not spare;*
> *The storm has swept our canvas almost bare.*
> *For this deficiency we will soon atone—*
> *Would you could build as fast with brick and stone.*

Mrs. William Thornton, wife of the Capitol's chief architect, found the season's performances "intolerably stupid." They continued for only a month. But crowds were large and included many distinguished figures: The executive officers had been in town since June, and along with the rest of the citizenry they were hungry for entertainment. Mrs. Thornton's tastes notwithstanding, the Chestnut Street Theater's stock acting company was the best in the land.

So Washington's theatre history begins with the best the nation has to offer, performed before some of its leading citizens on a makeshift stage in the grandly named "United States Theatre," actually the unfinished wing of a hotel destined never to be completed. An early resident named Christian Hines remembered sneaking into the theatre with other boys by lifting loose floorboards and climbing up from the basement. Clearly the capital needed a more permanent playhouse if its cultural aspirations were to match its political ambitions.

The first building erected specifically to be a playhouse opened in 1804 at 11th and C Streets, NW, on land donated by civic leader Major John P. Van Ness. It was named, predictably enough, the Washington Theatre. Little survives in the way of description. An Englishman labeled it "a miserable little rope-walking theatre," referring to the tightrope acrobatics popular at the time. But managers and performers had their own reasons for wanting to play Washington, theatre conditions aside. The city had its rough edges, but Washington offered something as alluring in its own way as money: an audience of the powerful. In addition to the Philadelphia Company and local thespians, touring stars from England played the house, which was

Star of the National's first season, French ballet artist Celine Celeste then spoke little English and performed only dance and pantomime, often in male roles such as the Arab Boy in The French Spy *(left) and the Pirate Boy in* The Wizard Skiff. *She branched into English-speaking parts later in her long career.*

attended by General Andrew Jackson, and by James Monroe and his family on the first recorded presidential visit to a theatre in Washington on March 26, 1819.

The building survived the burning of the city by British troops in August, 1814, and "The Star Spangled Banner" was sung there on July 4, 1815. As if in belated reckoning, the building caught fire from a cause unknown on the morning of April 19, 1820. Within a six-month period the Washington Theatre, the Chestnut Street in Philadelphia, and the Park Theatre in New York all burned. Fire was a constant companion to 19th-century urban life, and, as was the case in cities all over the country, signed an end to many chapters of Washington's theatre history. But more important, each fiery end also marked another beginning. And never in the course of Washington's theatre history has a fire taken a human life.

In 1822 another theatre named the Washington opened, this time on Louisiana Avenue between 4&½ and 6th Streets, NW. It was an improvement on the 23

original, with seats for 700 and good acoustics, though still no rival to Philadelphia's magnificently rebuilt Chestnut Street Theatre, or to the competition that had by then sprung up in that city at the Walnut Street Theatre. Built as a circus in 1809 and first used for theatre two years later, the Walnut Street is still active today as the oldest surviving playhouse in the country.

Gaetani Carusi, an Italian bandmaster who had come to Washington in 1805 to head the Marine Corps Band at Thomas Jefferson's request, bought the former Washington Theatre's site and erected the Washington Assembly Rooms, later called Carusi's Saloon. Here met the Washington Assembly—the ballroom dancing association of the elite—and other entertainments were sometimes held. The new Washington Theatre, however, led the city's theatrical life.

Some of the best talent found on this side of the Atlantic appeared there. Joseph Jefferson I, an English immigrant who became America's favorite comedian and founded one of the nation's great stage dynasties, played both the first and second Washington Theatres. His son, Joseph Jefferson II, less famous for his acting but noted as a scenery painter and manager, took over management of the second Washington Theatre in 1831. Four years later he appeared at the National Theatre on its opening night with the Chestnut Street Theatre company. His son, Joseph Jefferson III, in turn made his stage debut at the Washington Theatre at age four in 1833, when blackface comedian T.D. Rice emptied the youngster from a sack he had carried onstage. Dressed and made up identically to the six-foot originator of the ''Jim Crow'' part, the diminutive Jefferson mimicked every step of Rice's dance. A shower of coins rewarded the pair, and Joe Jefferson III was hooked on theatre for life.

Later he managed the National Theatre and went on to become one of America's most beloved actors with his own version of Rip Van Winkle, a part that brought him fame and supported him the rest of his life.

Another emigre giant of the American stage, Junius Brutus Booth, made his first appearance at the Washington Theatre on August 1, 1822, in the part of Richard III. One of his sons, Edwin Booth, played the same role in his Washington debut at the National Theatre 34 years later, a year before his first important appearance in New York. The first American-born tragedian to win major approval in Europe, Edwin Booth would reign as leading star of the American stage through most of the second half of the 19th Century, retiring two years before his death in 1893.

Edwin's older brother, Junius Brutus, Jr., became a successful manager and director in New York. The talented family's younger brother also launched a successful career as an actor, although he would never

English-born comedian William E. Burton revived the National's flagging first season with a variety of comic characters in well-received farces, many of which he wrote himself.

Tragedian Edwin Forrest was foremost in earning respect on both sides of the Atlantic for native-born American actors. He brought his "heroic, muscular style" to Shakespearean roles, such as King Lear, and to parts as Romans, Indians, and other classical and historical figures. An audience at the National once rushed the stage in outrage when members of the theatre's stock company supporting Forrest forgot their lines.

receive the acclaim given Edwin. On April 11, 1863, Abraham Lincoln looked on from the National Theatre's presidential box when John Wilkes Booth made his Washington debut as Richard III. Two years later the youngest of the theatrical Booth brothers was shot to death in a burning barn in Virginia twelve days after assassinating Lincoln at Ford's Theatre.

American-born tragedian Edwin Forrest, Yankee-character player James H. Hackett (first American actor to star in London), London-trained James Wallack the elder (another dynasty founder), and French dancer and pantomimist Mademoiselle Celine Celeste all played the second Washington Theatre. Presidents Monroe and John Quincy Adams, General Jackson and the Marquis de Lafayette attended. Remodeling in 1831 made room for 1,000 spectators and added coffee rooms and furnace heating. British actor Tyrone Power wrote in 1834 that "it was filled nightly with a very delightful audience."

But business overall left much to be desired. Certain incidents point to the kind of problems Jefferson and other managers faced: On the theatre's reopening after renovations, gas lamps that he installed did not work, and the audience had to be sent home. Some winter nights found the theatre too cold for actors or audience to bear, and shows were cancelled. In 1833 Jefferson wrote to the city council asking that the Negro curfew be amended so that blacks could attend his theatre. He estimated $10 in lost business per night, a burden borne on top of a $6 nightly performance tax. (Manager Francis Courtney Wemyss had made only $6 a week when he opened the theatre for two months in 1823.)

Visitors other than Power gave an altogether different picture of the theatre. In 1830 English traveller Frances Trollope found it "very small, and most astonishingly dirty and void of decoration, considering that it is the only place of amusement that the city affords." Fanny Kemble, an English actress who played the theatre in 1833, had an even stronger reaction: "The proprietors are poor, the actors poorer; and the grotesque mixture of misery, vulgarity, stage-finery, and real raggedness, is beyond anything strange and sad, and revolting."

Both Mesdames Trollope and Kemble published accounts of their American travels that took often disdainful, supercilious views of what was in fact the half-savage land of Jacksonian America, and their comments should be considered with that in mind. But the point was made that the nation's capital could not com-

Crowds braved sweltering summer heat to see leading tragedienne Ellen Tree. The National Intelligencer *reported that "She evinces soul, tact, manner and action. . . ."*

FOUNDING

The National's moment of conception occurred in August, 1834, when a stockholding company was formed and a board appointed to oversee the foundation of a new playhouse. It was intended to be closer to Georgetown and the President's Mansion (the President's House, as it was also called, did not become known as the White House until the 1850's) than the existing Washington Theatre on Louisiana Avenue. The seed had in fact been planted a few years earlier by a committee of prominent citizens chosen to petition Congress and the President for a lot on which to erect in Washington "a theatre which should be a monument of its taste, and of the liberality of its citizens." Nothing came of the move, but this spirit was revived by the company of 1834.

From the start theatre in Washington had enjoyed the patronage of the city's most respectable circles. Members of the National's founding board, leading citizens all, included William Brent; Cornelius Mclean, Jr.; Henry Randall; Richard Smith; and J. George Gibson. Brent, the brother of Washington's first mayor and a one-time candidate himself (Mclean, too, was once put forward as candidate for mayor), had served on the board of directors that founded the first Washington Theatre in 1804.

Better remembered in present-day Washington than any of these, however, through both his name and his works, was another pillar of the early community who brought the National through a critical juncture when some of the first subscribers failed to make good on their pledges. Son of a former mayor of Georgetown, William Wilson Corcoran was a businessman-turned-financier trying to sort out the debts of the United States Bank in 1834, when the new theatre project ran into the first setback in what was to be a history of harrowing financial crises.

Corcoran would reap a fortune during the Mexican-American War selling U.S. government bonds to Europeans, who had theretofore scorned the country's paper issue. He was an empire-builder in the age of Manifest Destiny who enlisted European investment in the task of settling and developing the vast new tracts of Western lands conquered from Mexico. A life-long Washingtonian, whose mansion stood at Connecticut and H Street, Corcoran was co-founder of Riggs Bank and one of the city's most generous philanthropists: Washington's oldest private art museum, a gift from the financier-cum-art-patron, bears his name. In biographical recitations of Corcoran's philanthropies and legacy to the city, his involvement with the National is often overlooked. But it was Corcoran who, in July, 1835, became owner of the theatre site for one day when the managers made the deed over to him. Corcoran then reconveyed it to the trustees, enabling the new theatre project to forge ahead.

pare in theatrical grandeur with the Republic's older, established leading cities. In an upstart newcomer city with imperial ambitions the lack must have been keenly felt. The unflattering contrast would have been especially rankling to the polished, monied lions of Washington society when pointed out by foreigners, and women at that.

The need for a better theatre certainly existed, and it is possible that Trollope's and Kemble's descriptions provided fresh motivation to found one. If so, then we should extend our thanks to the sharp-tongued pair as instigators of events that led to the notice in the *National Intelligencer* on December 4, 1835, announcing the opening on Monday, December 7, of a "new and splendid establishment . . . which for comfort, beauty, and magnificence, is equal if not superior, to any theatre in the country."

The National Theatre had arrived.

Earlier he had lent his voice in favor of the westerly location on Pennsylvania Avenue—an area destined to grow quickly into the city's downtown—when arguments were heard for building closer to already-developed Capitol Hill. His voice carried weight, and a notice in the *Intelligencer* of August 26, 1834, soliciting proposals for erecting the theatre (notices also appeared in Baltimore, Philadelphia, and New York) detailed plans to build on the triangular lot between the Avenue and 13th and E Streets. Joe Jefferson II was named as manager. Then the location was changed and two lots were purchased from John Mason on 13th Street facing Pennsylvania Avenue across the open triangular lot. (That triangle was never permanently built upon, and has come down the years as a sometimes dusty, sometimes green ornament to the Avenue. Today it is incorporated into a rectangular plaza newly landscaped as part of Pennsylvania Avenue's redevelopment.)

The National had arrived on the spot where it would still stand (albeit in its sixth structural incarnation) one and a half centuries later. Fifty years earlier, before the arrival of the federal government, the site had belonged to Davy Burnes, whose farm stretched from Capitol Hill (Jenkins' Hill, until the 1790's) to the knoll on which

the President's Mansion was built. Between that time and the National's construction, the block held a few brick and frame houses, a saloon, and, on the same location chosen for the theatre, a place of entertainment called the Rotunda.

The E Street location provided a handy place for carriages to line up off Pennsylvania Avenue. Taxis and limousines would later find it equally convenient. Getting to the theatre, however, was no easy task in 1835. The Avenue had been macadamized a few years earlier but was already returning to a miasmic state. Craters and hillocks of mud overturned carriages in mid-avenue. Pigs ran loose in the streets. In a history of the National Theatre written in 1885, entitled "New National Theatre, Washington D.C., A Record of Fifty Years," authors Alexander Hunter and J.H. Polkinhorn wrote that, at the National's founding, "slush was king, and mud monarch." Washington was "the most ill-conditioned city on the continent," and "a dead city, with no trade, and kept alive only by the money of the Government employees."

But if conditions in Jacksonian Washington were trying, Jacksonian Americans were a match for them, and although heat and cold frequently thinned audiences, the playhouse itself was all and more for which

NATIONAL THEATRE.—Mr. RICE, the celebrated imitator of negro characters, made his first appearance last Monday night before a not very large audience. At the end of the play, a very disgraceful scene occurred, in which certain females in the third tier of boxes conducted themselves with such outrageous indecorum, that they were immediately taken into custody by the police officers, and committed by a police magistrate, then present, to the workhouse, where they remained until the next day, when they found unexceptionable security for their good behaviour for one year.

In consequence of this outrage and other acts of indecorum, which have originated in the third tier of boxes, during the last week, and by which the feelings of the respectable part of the audience, and especially ladies, have been grievously annoyed, the manager has ordered the third tier of boxes to be closed, and made that announcement to the audience last Monday evening. We sincerely hope this act of the manager will be duly appreciated by the respectable portion of our fellow-citizens who patronize the drama. The same line of conduct pursued by the manager under similar circumstances in the Holiday street theatre, Baltimore, procured for him the most substantial proof of public favor; and in no moral or respectable community can it, in our opinion, fail to be otherwise. We are advocates of dramatic exhibitions only as they are unconnected with such impurities as no decent person or respectable female can bear to witness.

CIRCUIT COURT FOR THE DISTRICT OF COLUMBIA.—No criminal trials of more than ordinary character took place in this court during the last week, except on Saturday last, when a female of very respectable connexion in this city,

Ladies and gentlemen often appeared to be neither in their theatregoing manners during the Republic's early years. Even more unruly were the 25-cent patrons of the third tier, where "gallery gods"—young white rowdies—and unidentified "females" raised rows beside the "gallery for people of color."

Jacksonian Washington could have hoped.

The *National Intelligencer* thought so. Washingtonian Aloysius I. Mudd, who chronicled early D.C. theatre for the Columbia Historical Society in 1902, noticed that newspapers only gradually came to publish reviews of plays—a symptom, it seems, of the holdover ambivalence about theatre's respectability that prevailed in local churches. These feelings would surface again in 1865, when Lincoln's assassination in a theatre, at the hand of an actor, seemed to bear out their direst apprehensions. But the *Intelligencer*, published by Joseph Gales, Jr., and William Winston Seaton, Washington's leading daily until the *Evening Star*'s advent in 1852, was a supporter of the National Theatre from the start. On Friday, December 4, 1835, the following article appeared:

NATIONAL THEATRE

The lovers of the Drama will be gratified to learn that this new and beautiful theatre will certainly open on Monday next. The lessees (Messrs. MAYWOOD, ROWBOTHAM, and PRATT, the proprietors of the Chestnut Street Theatre, Philadelphia) have made the necessary arrangements for this purpose, and are confident that no disappointment to the public will occur. The construction of the theatre is admirable, both for its commodiousness and for seeing and hearing; the arrangement of the seats is very convenient, and the decorations will be elegant in every respect. The dome of the theatre is finished, and is the most beautiful thing of the kind I have seen, and when the house is lighted up the effect will be exceedingly brilliant. It is painted of a pale cerulean blue color, and is divided into four allegorical designs. The first represents the Genius of the Institutions of the Country, designated by Power and Wisdom repelling Tyranny and Superstition. The second represents Truth at the Altar, from which the spirits of War and Peace have taken the Sword and Torch. The third represents the Goddess of Wisdom presenting a medallion of WASHINGTON to the Genius of Liberty, who returns a wreath to crown her favorite son—Fame proclaiming Victory and Peace. The last represents Justice protecting and guiding the Commerce and Manufactures of America. The artist is a Mr. WHITE, from New York, and the genius he has displayed on the Dome, the Proscenium, the Drop Curtain, and on various portions of the decorations, will, I am sure, give general satisfaction; and it will add to the public gratification when it is discovered that the whole of the ornaments of the interior are of a national character, representing, either by allegorical designs or historical illustrations, important events in the history of the country. This is as it should be in a National Theatre.

Along the front of the first tier of boxes, connected with the parquet and probably on a level with the stage, imitation-bas-relief sketches and ornaments portrayed "brilliant events in the maritime history and discovery, and naval achievements." The second tier's heroic associations dwelt on "victories, treaties, agriculture, &c." More were clustered on the proscenium. On the arch, directly over the stage, "the wings of Time" supported a representation of the Declaration of Independence.

The curtain that opened and closed the evening's main shows and signalled ends and beginnings of acts pictured a statue of George Washington on horseback, and behind it draperies half-parted to reveal "the Tomb of Washington, Mount Vernon, &c." In addition to representing the theatre's particular theme (the word "National" was carved into the building's granite cornerstone) and reflecting the fervent worship of the "Father of His Country," the painted curtain indicates the first National's currency with a new style of its time, replacing the plain green curtain inherited from 18th-Century London tradition.

The layout of the interior was innovative, placing high-priced parquet seating in what had formerly been the "pit," and removing the pit's former regulars to the third-tier gallery. A feature from Elizabethan times, the pit at first had been literally that, an arena for cockfights, below the boxes and in front of the stage. No record of cockfighting in the early Washington theatres has been found, but the crowd that frequented their pits was a rough one at best. Frances Trollope scathingly characterized the audience at her one visit to Joe Jefferson's Washington Theatre:

"The Elssler" fascinated the theatregoing public with her dancing and her beauty on a two-year American tour that reaped the German-born artist a fortune. Her repertoire included the beautiful "Shadow Dance." Public adulation erupted in a hand-drawn carriage ride in Baltimore, mocked as excessive in a cartoon.

I have before mentioned the want of decorum at the Cincinnati theater, but certainly that of the capital at least rivalled it in the freedom of action and attitude; a freedom that seems to disdain the restraints of civilized manners. One man in the pit was seized with a violent fit of vomiting, which appeared not in the least to annoy or surprise his neighbors; and the happy coincidence of a physician being at the moment personated on the stage, was hailed by many of the audience as an excellent joke, of which the actor took advantage, and elicited shouts of applause by saying, "I expect my services are wanted elsewhere."

Such was the humor of the pit—and of the actors who played to it. Not that the higher-paying customers were necessarily more courtly: Mrs. Trollope further writes that "not one in ten of the illustrious legislative audience sat according to the usual custom of human beings; the legs were thrown sometimes over the front of the box, sometimes over the side of it; here and there a senator stretched his entire length along the bench, and in many instances the front rail was preferred as a seat."

These precedents explain the implied message in the reviewer's statement that the parquet was "so fitted up that it will be equally desirable for the ladies to frequent the lower boxes. . . . As the convenience and the gratification of the ladies have been consulted on the occasion, I have no doubt that the Parquet and the lower boxes will exhibit a brilliant array of beauty and elegance on the opening." He was appealing to the ladies of fashion for their support. Two days after the opening night, the same reviewer wrote that "the experiment has succeeded."

A saloon behind the second level of boxes served coffee, fruit, and confectionary, although no doubt stronger beverages were sipped in the gallery and perhaps the boxes too. "New and splendid lamps" were supplied by the nation's leading lamp-maker, Mr. Cornelius of Philadelphia, who also lit the Capitol building. Artist John Carr was the new theatre's scenery painter, and one Mr. Varden created the stage machinery. The stage was strong enough to bear the weight of horses for the equestrian acts so popular in that era of horsemanship, and the parquet seats and flooring could be removed to create an amphitheater for circus performances.

The building was of Roman Doric style stuccoed in imitation of granite, fronting E Street for 76½ feet with five large doors and the same number of windows. A portico 41½ feet long stood 12 feet 9 inches out from

the building's front, supported by four brick pillars 29½ feet high complete with antae, entablature, and ballustrade. The building ran back 150 feet from E Street, standing 50 feet high atop a basement 13½ feet deep. Little more is known of the first theatre, but the *Intelligencer's* eyewitness descriptions give us enough to picture a handsome, stylish establishment that would have been a welcome addition to the architecture of Pennsylvania Avenue as well as to the evening life along it.

The *Intelligencer's* reviewer remarked as much in his pre-opening notice, writing, "In truth, it is only justice to say that the stockholders have endeavored so to construct the Theatre as to meet the wishes and wants of all classes of the community." The following week, after the Monday night opening of the National on December 7, 1835, he found his predictions at least initially fulfilled:

> This new and magnificent establishment opened for performance Monday evening to a very full house. The parquet and the boxes were filled with Ladies and Gentlemen, and the *tout ensemble* must have formed a highly gratifying *coup d'oeil* to the spirited manager—a precursor, it is hoped, of what he may expect through the season, provided he realizes the assurances and promises he has made. . . . Go on, Gentleman Managers, pursue a liberal policy toward your Stock Company, let the Stars you have promised emit their radiance in due season, always keep faith with the public, and you will never have occasion to appear as 'Managers in Distress.' On the contrary, you will gather a harvest of professional laurels, and be cheered in your course not merely by empty applause, but thousands of golden eagles will hover round you, and settle down in the capacious 'silk netted purses' with which you are doubtless provided.

Beginning with Thomas Ward, acting and stage manager for Maywood's Chestnut Street Theatre troupe at the National's opening, a long string of managers—women as well as men—would bring star performers and every manner of popular entertainment to the National in what was throughout most of the antebellum era a fruitless search for the key to financial success. Politics and its attendant social whirl competed with the theatre for society's allegiance. Appealing but high-salaried stars filled the seats but reaped scant profits for theatre managers. Cold in winter and heat in summer blighted attendance, and the rapid succession of managers in the first decades suggests that while "golden eagles" may have hovered around their en-

deavors, precious few settled into their silk netted purses.

But the National, once launched, would struggle on through bankruptcy, fire, and disaster, always reopening again at the E Street address. The founding stockholders must have wondered from time to time, as their investment reaped them little but loss, what had gone awry in their grand dreams. Authors Hunter and Polkinhorn, in their history of the first 50 years, answer that question with words that ring even more true today, a century after they were written: "Their judgement was vindicated by time, but not in their time; yet they builded for posterity better than they knew."

FIRST SEASON

The National opened on the same day as the first session of the 24th Congress, yet even so the lamps on Pennsylvania Avenue were unlit. A member of Congress wrote the *Intelligencer* a few weeks later in outrage over this civic penny-pinching, "I can scarcely tell when I am safe, the hacks buzzing about, and the mud so thick that, if I attempt to shun them, I am in it, and no light to direct me out."

Facing the darkness of this uncouth national thoroughfare, the National Theatre would have blazed with lights as the Chestnut Street Theatre company performed Charles Macklin's *Man of the World*, with theatre lessee R.C. Maywood in the leading role of Sire Pertinax Macsychophant. This pseudo-Restoration piece, thick with 18th-Century Scottish dialect, is deservedly obscure today, and even in 1835 was seldom performed. But the evening's bill was well-received, beginning with an address written by H. Penrose Vose of Baltimore, invoking the goddess of Liberty speaking from the Capitol dome:

Decorum departed with the guests of honor at an inaugural ball for President James K. Polk, when revelers at the National swarmed for food and drink. The chaos was reenacted at evening's end, when hats and cloaks were found to be missing. Fire destroyed the first National Theatre on the following evening.

"Here, in the city of my chosen son,
The Godlike, the immortal WASHINGTON,
Long may the drama act its powerful part,
T'instruct the mind, and elevate the heart."

In addition to the Chestnut Street and the National theatres, Maywood and Co. also operated playhouses in Annapolis and Baltimore. Railroad service linking Washington with Baltimore began in 1835, and this improved access, combined with Maywood's booking abilities, delivered a full and lively season featuring some of the best talent in the country.

On the third night of performances, popular London-trained James Wallack and a young American-born actress, Emma Wheatley, initiated with *Hamlet* the long roster of Shakespearean dramas that would appear at the National. Antebellum theatrical circuits were dominated by the "Star System": well-known performers with established repertoires traveling widely, supported in each town by the local stock company. The system was alternately the bane and salvation of theatre managers. Stars often filled auditoriums, but they commanded fees and percentages that local managements were hard-pressed to meet when crowds failed to materialize. Cold weather and the holiday social schedule left the early National noticeably empty in the pre-Christmas weeks, and the announcement for *Hamlet* emphasizes that "additional and efficient means have been taken to render the Theatre warm as well as comfortable. . . ." This would be a seasonal litany for many years to come.

On Christmas Eve, brief competition began when the renovated Washington Theatre reopened as the American Theatre, but lasted only until February. It was this old theatre's last season. In the meantime the National's nascent fortunes improved. The "celebrated low comedian" William E. Burton, an Englishman who would later manage the National, became an instant favorite, filling houses between Christmas and New Year. A few days later a rope dancer, Herr Cline, drew crowds to "View the steadiness and ease with which he performs evolutions the most extraordinary and beautiful. . . ." Among other feats, Herr Cline walked up a rope from stage to third tier while pushing a wheelbarrow, performed dances in wooden shoes and on stilts on both taut and slack ropes, and caused an uproar of approval when, dressed as Mercury, he balanced his way up to the third-tier gallery to visit his "fellow gods."

Appropriately enough for the self-consciously "national" theatre, one of the most active figures in its early days was George Washington's adopted grandson, George Washington Parke Custis. Master of the mansion that overlooks Washington today from its hilltop in Arlington Cemetery, Custis lost no opportunity to present on the National's stage his work as a playwright of historical themes. The first season saw performances of *Pocohantas, or the Settlers of Virginia*; *Montgomerie, or the Orphan of the Wreck*; and *The Launch of the Columbia, or America's Bluejackets Forever*, a light piece celebrating the then-current construction of the warship *Columbia* at the Washington Navy Yard. A song written by Custis celebrating the Battle of New Orleans was sung on the battle's January 8 anniversary, and an ode to George Washington was read on his birthday—then one of the most celebrated national holidays.

The Commissioner of the Indian Bureau and another private collector loaned Indian costumes for *Pocohantas*. "A friend, who feels much interested in this national drama," reported that "The principle scene of the piece is the rescue of the renowned Captain Smith by the Indian princess—an incident of such remarkable inter-

31

Jenny Lind was the toast of her time, inspiring advertisers to capitalize on her popularity. Bodies of opinion opposed to the theatre envisioned an evil influence in P.T. Barnum's hugely successful promotion campaign (below), one that made the "Swedish Nightingale" a household phrase.

est, that poetry, painting, and sculpture have all exerted their powers to do it homage."

This extravaganza was emulated by another patriotic playwright, General Alexander Macomb, commander of the U.S. Army, with *Pontiac, or the Siege of Detroit*. The General's dramatic effort enlisted members of the Marine Corps as extras, and was remembered fifty years later by eyewitnesses as a "lurid and bewildering display of rapidly shifting scenes, volleys of musketry, heaps of dead Indians, &c."

Custis's son-in-law, a young U.S. Army officer named Robert E. Lee, became a stockholder in the National Theatre in its antebellum days.

Junius Brutus Booth, the rival of Edwin Forrest for the title of America's leading tragedian, added to the National's prestige with appearances as Richard III and other Shakespearian roles, including a King Lear performed "in consequences of numerous and pressing solicitations from members of Congress and others." Booth was then at the height of his powers both in drama and dissipation. Ben Perley Poore, author of *Perley's Reminiscences*, wrote of the era, "Booth, at this time, was more than ever the slave to intoxicating drink, so much so that he would often disappoint his audiences, sometimes wholly failing to appear, yet his popularity remained unabated."

But the season's star performer was neither English nor American, and rarely played a speaking part. The New World was eschewed as a cultural wasteland by most European stars, but Madame Celine Celeste discovered here a financial golden lode. With her talent for pantomime and dance she captivated New York in 1827, just as she had previously beguiled Paris and London.

In 1836, playing a series of melodramatic pieces written expressly for her, she broke all box office records, receiving some $50,000 in a year's time. She arrived in Washington from a New Orleans engagement reported to be the most profitable ever known in America, with receipts for 24 nights averaging $1,028.50. So high were her fees that seats in the National's first tier of boxes and parquet section, which soon after the theatre's opening had been reduced in the face of scanty houses from $1 to 75 cents, went back to $1.

No grumbles were heard, however, from a public ready to worship her. Rather plain-looking, Celeste adopted exotic costumes, often playing a man or boy and appearing in three or four roles in plays such as *The Wizard Skiff, or, The Tongueless Pirate Boy*; *The Death Plank, or, A True Tale of the Sea*, and others whose titles evoke similar melodramatic themes and settings. As the first European ballerina to cross the Atlantic, her victorious march from Montreal to New Orleans presaged later triumphs by Fanny Elssler and others. Nationwide adulation of Celeste amounted to America's first theatrical fad, and admiration by members of President Jackson's administration was so ardent that they were satirized in the election campaign as the "Celestal-Cabinet."

On her benefit night, the customary climax of a star's engagement, when all proceeds went directly to the artist, the largest crowd in the National's brief history jammed the theatre, "the house literally overflowing from the bottom to the top, and yet hundreds went away without being able to get in." The program included the melodramatic pantomime, *The Wept of Wish-ton-wish*, drawn from James Fennimore Cooper's novel *The Borderers*, in which "The parting scene with her Conanchet, the delight she displayed upon hearing his voice, and the recovery of her reason from the effects of music, were all beautifully expressed. Her dying scene is also very fine."

Celeste, who married a Baltimore native, played and managed theatres on both sides of the Atlantic for many years and returned often to the National, remaining popular as she judiciously modified her styles of dancing to best accommodate her advancing years. But her National debut, when Washington audiences showed what they were prepared to do for a star they idolized, was never surpassed.

The patriotic theme of the National's decor was underscored by a new drop curtain installed late in the season, "representing a brilliant landscape in a rich frame of arabesque Basso Relievo, with medallions, in which are faithful portraits of the Presidents of the United States; George Washington, the Father of his Country, Adams, Jefferson, Madison, Monroe, John Q. Adams, and Andrew Jackson. At the base of which is a beautiful entablature displaying the Sacrifice of Prejudice at the altar of Truth."

It was an era of great national events, and happenings on the National's stage reflect the concerns of the time. As the first season progressed, newspaper accounts appearing alongside the theatre's advertising chronicled at first contradictory, then grimly substantiated reports of a massacre beyond America's borders at a place called the Alamo. On May 4, while Sam Houston awaited Santa Anna on the River Brassos, a stock company actress at the National sang *Huzza for Liberty and Texas*, "a new patriotic song . . . written by J. Dickson, Esq. (himself a sufferer in the cause)."

In Florida, a possession but not yet a state, Seminoles were waging a peppery and at that point successful campaign against white settlers. In January a Cherokee delegation visiting Washington accepted an invitation from manager Ward to see the evening's comedy, and their attendance was advertised in the newspaper. The Trail of Tears, when the Cherokees would be herded west of the Mississippi or hunted through their Southern forests, was a few years yet in the future.

In Washington itself, a Southern town governed by the U.S. Congress, the most hotly debated local issue was the attempt, eventually successful, to halt slave sales in Center Market, a few blocks down Pennsyl- 33 vania Avenue from the theatre. Blacks could sit in the "Gallery for persons of color" for 25 cents, the same price paid by the white "gallery gods."

The stiffest competition the National faced was Washington's raison d'etre, sport, and principal preoccupation: politics, and the social life that from Washington's beginnings had been so much of a piece with politics' ceaseless maneuvering. Newspaper notices stress that the evening performances, which usually began at 6:30, would end by 10 o'clock, enabling busy citizens to relax from the cares of the day but still attend the evening's social business.

An evening's fare typically began with a full-length tragedy, comedy, or melodrama, followed by a musical farce, then a "fancy dance" or hornpipe, magic tricks or feats of acrobatics and gymnastics, and concluded almost invariably with a farce to send the audience home laughing. On May 14, 1836, Ward presented a comedy, a farewell address, a violin solo, and a farce entitled *Green Eyed Monster* to end the season with a chuckle.

Race Week had begun, a holiday time when neither the Senate nor the House could muster a quorum as members flocked to horse races in what is now Foggy Bottom. Theatre manager Ward could enjoy the races while looking back with some satisfaction on the season: He had presented some of the most famous actors on the continent, including Celeste, the day's leading box-office draw, and backed them with members of the nation's best stock company. The National counted among its stockholders the wealthiest and most influential citizens of the city, and had several times been used for the city's most elite and ceremonious social occasions, the balls held by the Washington Assembly.

There had been some poor nights, both in fullness of house and quality of performance. But there was also much of the best. In the simple concept of excellence lies the secret of the National's unique and phenomenal survival as a leading stage for the nation.

EARLY YEARS

The violinist from Norway, Ole Bull, held the audience in the palm of his hand until the congressman from Alabama became obstreperous. Poore tells us that "while every breath was suspended, and every ear attentive to catch the sounds of his magical instrument," the star was interrupted by General Felix Grundy McConnell, representing Alabama's Talladega District, shouting "None of your high-falutin', but give us 'Hail Columbia,' and bear hard on the treble!"

The general was reportedly one of the most athletic men in the 1842 Congress, and it took the policemen, who were often present at National, no little time to subdue and carry him from the theatre. The Congressman's friends later prevailed on management to allow him back in for the rest of the show.

It is little wonder that newspaper playbills gave frequent assurances that police would be in attendance. For if this was the behavior of congressmen in the 75-cent seats, what could be expected from the two-bit customers in the gallery?

Decorum did not prevail in the third tier. A Philadelphia theatre manager deplored chandelier lighting because it lit "that very portion which should be kept as much as possible in the shade . . . the third tier of boxes, where licentiousness prevails in its worst form."

At the National trouble cropped up early in the second season with frequent disturbances. Following a performance by blackface comedian T.D. Rice there erupted "a very disgraceful scene . . . in which certain females in the third tier of boxes conducted themselves with such outrageous indecorum" that they were arrested and later ordered on good behavior for a year.

To assuage growing public reaction, manager Ward closed the gallery, but not for long. Newsworthy acts of outrageousness continued to occur there (and in other parts of the theatre) throughout the National's early years. From time to time, "females" were barred from the third tier, presumably due to an influx of painted ladies from the bawdy houses on the other side of the Avenue.

At the front door "gangs of disorderly and turbulent lads" annoyed playgoers by begging "checks" for entry. At the evening's end hack drivers rushed the entrance "regardless of the limbs and lives of those who are their customers" necessitating the presence of a constable to control traffic.

There are no reports of disorder in the colored gallery, which had, however, for a time its own social stratification: a 50-cent section was set aside for "respectable persons of color" separate from the 25-cent seats.

There was much on the boards to please "gallery gods" of all caste. Low humor, caricature, and slapstick were staples of the day, along with acrobatic and oddity acts. The Ravel family were pantomimists, gymnasts, and rope dancers who gave "thrilling performances in air and on unsteady foundations of all sorts." The Wild Bedouin Arabs performed a "Grand Ballet of Action" most frequently described in newspaper accounts as astonishing. Hervio Nano, "a monkey imitator of unrivalled powers and prowess," impersonated a fly as well as a baboon in pieces that also starred the misshapen performer in the role of an ape. In an appearance billed as her first on any stage, the acrobatic Herr Cline's grandmother danced with him a *pas de deux*.

On a more intellectual plane, the omniscient Dr. Lardner, editor of the Cabinet Encyclopedia, displayed knowledge of that very sort with lectures, illustrated by transparencies, dioramas, models, and machines, explicating the eye, waterspouts, electricity, the power of steam, and steam navies of the U.S. and Britain, as well as the sun and moon, Mars, Jupiter, Saturn, Hal-

Oddity was an asset for novelty stars, among whom the stump-legged Hervio Nano (top) embodied one of the more bizarre successes. Acrobats and gymnasts, the Ravel Family and Herr Cline performed their feats of balance and agility in the course of presenting songs, dances, skits, farces, and pantomimes.

ley's Comet, the aurora borealis, life on other planets and, not least intriguing, "popular fallacies."

The Tattooed Man, Mr. O'Connell, a "modern Robinson Crusoe" from Dublin who had been shipwrecked in the North Pacific and tattooed by a tribe there, exhibited, in addition to his decorated skins, "astonishing feats of agility in Dancing, which was the means of saving his life when landed on a barbarous coast."

Mr. Porter the "Kentucky Giant," 7 feet nine inches tall, and Major Stevens, who stood 40 inches, appeared in *Tom Thumb* and *Lilliputians in Kentucky.* In the latter production, Porter played a half-grown Kentucky hunter and Major Stevens a banished nobleman from Lilliput.

Monsieur Paul, the Modern Hercules, strained against four horses while riders urged them on with whips. "Equestrian dramas," featuring trained horses and feats of riding, included *Mazeppa, or the Wild Horse of Tartary*, enormously popular for many years, and *Timour the Tartar*, "with every accessible aid of scenery, dresses, banners, armor suits, war weapons, combats, processions, and magnificent tableaux in addition to a complete Stud of Beautiful Horses."

An act involving trained lions and tigers disappointingly failed to arrive, and "when last heard from, were stuck in the snow about 8 miles this side of Philadelphia."

In every season, however, more conventional stars and troupes furnished the main bill of fare. Burton was always a hit, the paper advising "all those who suffer low spirits and ennui" to go and see him. Comedian Tyrone Power presented Irish characters, and Yankee Hill his caricatured New Englanders of rustic virtues and native wit.

Leading tragedians Abbott, Vandenhoff, and Addams appeared. Celeste returned many times, as did Junius Brutus Booth, who played at least once at the National with President Van Buren in the audience.

President Van Buren and many other government leaders also attended the first National appearance of Edwin Forrest, Booth's rival and the leading American-born tragedian. Unfortunately the National's stock company supported him with uneven levels of competence: one actress was actually led from the stage after butchering Desdemona and another role. On the whole, however, Forrest's initial engagement was a triumph: Leading families bought seats for every night of his week-long appearance, and on the evening when Van Buren attended, receipts peaked with a record $1,030.

James H. Hackett failed in the part of Richard III after publishing an article criticizing other leading stars' interpretations of the part and championing his own reading of the character. After a single performance he followed a critic's advice that he retreat to comedy parts, for which he was beloved.

A sweltering June brought leading Shakespearian ac-

tress Ellen Tree to present "a perfect piece of acting, superior to anything we have witnessed on the stage for the last twenty years." She played to good houses despite furnace-like conditions that forced some fans to leave an hour into her performance.

The unquestioned champion of female performers on the first National's boards was German danseuse Fanny Elssler, who captivated the capital and, indeed, the nation in 1840. Touring the sights of Washington, she was honored when the Senate rose as she entered its chamber, and the House insisted on seating her in the Speaker's chair. At the National, men stood in the aisles and on steps to see her perform. (All ladies present had seats.) One viewer declared that simply to see her sit in a chair was worth the price of admission. "The loveliness of her undraped limbs" and "her exquisite poetry of motion" brought the audience to its feet at the end of her premiere performance, and bouquets were flung onto the stage. Hunter and Polkinhorn wrote that women stripped off their jewelry and men their rings and watch chains to fling them onto the stage as Elssler "stood a veritable Danae in this shower of gold."

Despite the homage paid to foreign stars, patriotic notes were often sounded on special occasions. The National's company opened the second season on December 7, 1836, by singing as a "National Anthem," a pre-Irving Berlin "God Bless America." They repeated the performance on Washington's Birthday. "The Star Spangled Banner" was also sung at the first National, and the Marine Corps Band sometimes accompanied performances.

Managers lost no opportunity to entice the public by

A charming adventuress, Irish-born Maria Dolores Eliza Rosanna Gilbert cited Spanish heritage in adopting the name Lola Montez. Admired by the Czar of Russia and the King of Bavaria, she parlayed scandalous notoriety in Europe into popular attention in the New World when she crossed the Atlantic after being banished from Bavaria. Her dancing skills were reputedly not great.

LOLA COMING!

EUROPE FAREWELL! AMERICA I COME.

advertising spectacular shows and, on occasion, distinguished patrons. An announcement in 1842 erroneously predicted Charles Dickens's attendance at an evening of comedy. Publicity for *St. George and the Dragon* promised a spectacle that had cost $3,000 to stage. There is no indication whether or not this expense was recouped, but repeated pleas in the *Intelligencer* for greater public support of the National suggest that if the show was a loss, this was by no means unusual. While audiences were often dazzling in their pre-eminence, and stars usually enhanced attendance, day-to-day support was not sufficient for financial success. Troupes went wherever returns were best, and the National was frequently dark. An 1842 guidebook to the city predicted the National's imminent closing, and the *Intelligencer* exhorted, "Washingtonians, arouse! support your stationary Theatre, instead of the ephemeral gewgaws and puppet shows with which our city is overrun."

Thomas Ward was joined by a co-manager, Mr. Walton, but the two were soon succeeded by Virginia Monier—the first of two female managers in the National's history, both during the antebellum years. Ward frequently returned from managing theatres in Baltimore and elsewhere to reopen the National, but he performed his last labors in Washington in 1843. With his departure events turned truly disastrous.

A manager named Hield, along with Messrs. Collins, Tuthill and Donaldson, reopened the theatre in 1843 after repairing and repainting the auditorium and installing new lamps. It closed within weeks. The *Intelligencer* described one performance under this management as "ludicrous," and Hunter and Polkinhorn reported that on another occasion "Miss Palm and Mister Sinclair absolutely emptied the house, by their lugubrious acting of that dismal drama, *The Stranger*." These unfortunate actors' baggage was seized by their hotel in lieu of payment, and the *Intelligencer* commented that they were lucky to escape town with their lives.

This seeming nadir in the theatre's fortunes would be exceeded in 1852, when a manager departed Washington abruptly, leaving behind $200 in bad debts.

L.M. Emery from Baltimore tried his hand after Hield, but he too was forced to close. Early in 1843 the theatre was transformed into a circus, with the parquet and orchestra removed to form an amphitheatre. The circus season, with an India Rubber Man as a star attraction, was a short one.

In 1844 stockholders took a beating when the theatre, which had cost more than $40,000 to erect, was sold for $13,500 to leading citizens General Van Ness, Benjamin Ogle Tayloe, and Richard Smith.

Briefly leased by a Mr. Rodney, then abandoned, the National was rescued again by Washington favorite William E. Burton, who leased the theatre early in 1845. The season's high point came not onstage but in the auditorium, cleared of seats for an inaugural ball honoring President James K. Polk. Another ball held simultaneously at Carusi's Saloon, with admission costing $10, attracted the cream of Washington society, while the National's five-dollar entry fee drew the local Democratic Party rank-and-file. The new President and his notoriously strait-laced wife made an awkward appearance during which the rambunctious throng in the National's auditorium momentarily ceased drinking and the music was silenced. Moments after the Polks left, the guests attacked the food and drink set out on banquet tables.

Perley says that the "fight for the supper was emblematical of the scramble about to be made for the loaves and fishes of office." Later, when guests began to leave, they discovered that many of the best hats, cloaks, and canes had been purloined from the cloakroom.

On March 5, 1845, the night following the ball, a fire broke out in the National's oil room in the midst of a performance by the "Congo Melodists," a minstrel group from Boston. Everyone in the building escaped unharmed, but despite the arrival of fire-fighting companies from as far away as Alexandria, the concerted efforts of patrons, firemen, and actors were unable to save the structure when water froze in the hoses.

Several nearby buildings also burned, and the National was left a blackened shell. No insurance was carried on the building, and for the next five years the site remained empty save for ruins.

THE SWEDISH NIGHTINGALE

No previous popular phenomenon matched the adulation with which America received Jenny Lind, the Swedish Nightingale, when she crossed the Atlantic in 1850. She arrived under the entrepreneurial management of P.T. Barnum, father of the modern advertising blitz. Renowned for her voice, her serenity, and her devotion to charity (a quality Barnum lost no opportunity to exploit), Lind did not know that Barnum's

ENTHUSIASTIC RECEPTION OF LOLA BY AN AMERICAN AUDIENCE.

canny advance campaign had unleashed a national frenzy that would come to be known as Lind-o-mania.

Several foreign stars had earlier captivated the American public, but Barnum took promotions to a new level, orchestrating anticipation of the event with a success that promoters could envy today. Lind herself was unprepared for the New World's riotous reception. Crowds met her on the pier in New York and admiring throngs gathered below her hotel window to serenade her. On her arrival by train in Baltimore, young male admirers took the traces of her carriage and pulled her through the streets. Products ranging in appropriateness from sheet music to chewing tobacco were renamed after her, and women performers gained a new respectability in American eyes due to Lind's well-publicized aura of wholesomeness. Men and women surged into her concerts, happy to pay whatever Barnum thought the traffic would bear.

Yet Jenny Lind's presence on American shores brought consternation in Washington. With the National gone, the capital of America's 23 million people had no hall large and gracious enough in which to present the toast of the nation to its most prominent citizens. Barnum grandly requested the Capitol building itself for his concert hall. Its acquisition would have been a master stroke for the great showman, but Congressional rules prevented it.

Instead, once again, Washington businessmen filled the breach. Willard of Willard's Hotel and mail-coach magnate "Land Admiral" Reeside purchased the National's ruins and rebuilt on the spot, incorporating portions of the old building's still-standing brick walls into a new structure to accommodate an audience of 3,500. It was advertised as the "new National Hall." Architect Robert Mills inspected the building and wrote that its two-foot-thick masonry could support "any possible weight of persons collected within its walls."

The interior was still unfinished and redolent of fresh plaster and paint when Lind made an uncharacteristically quiet arrival in Washington by train on December 15, 1850. The Lind-Barnum entourage took rooms at the Willard Hotel (Willard's stylish establishment was a newcomer among Pennyslvania Avenue accommodations), where President Millard Fillmore came to call. The singer was away, but she returned the visit the next day at the President's Mansion. Here she and Barnum were received by the amiable Chief Executive and his wife, whose comfortable manner put their European visitor at ease. Lind asked, in the course of conversation, how the American people were governed. "Our people govern themselves, mostly," Fillmore replied, "which does not leave much for the President to do." He is reported to have remarked years later that Lind's visit to Washington was the most exciting event of his presidency.

Washington's elite, for their part, put on their best show. Lind was ushered into both houses of Congress in session and heard Henry Clay argue a case before the Supreme Court. Secretary of State Daniel Webster received her in his offices at the Treasury Building—the senior statesman was a devoted fan who attended Lind's concerts in several cities. At Mount Vernon, where she journeyed by steamer for an afternoon, Colonel John A. Washington, great-great-nephew of the first president, presented the singer with a book from George Washington's library, with notes in the great man's hand.

The most impressive tribute rendered, however, was in the makeup of the audiences who filled National Hall on December 16 and 18. Both nights' turnouts included the President and Mrs. Fillmore, their family, the entire Cabinet, Supreme Court justices, and such national heroes as Senator Clay and General Winfield Scott. Tickets ranged from $3 to $7 even though new wooden seats had warped due to hasty construction. Temporary bannisters and steps of rough boards had been erected, and many gas lights lacked glass covers.

Armchairs were placed in the best section of the orchestra for the President and other luminaries. The overture at the first concert was repeatedly interrupted by applause for Webster, Clay, and others as they individually made grand entrances from the auditorium door to the overstuffed chairs in front.

Daniel Webster gave the most remarkable performance of all at the second concert. He and a number of other cabinet members had been dinner guests of the Russian envoy, who was noted for his generosity with refreshments. Webster led the group somewhat unsteadily into the auditorium while Lind was in mid-performance. Soon after, the "Sweet Ambassadress of Song," as Barnum billed Lind on her Washington visit, performed "Hail Columbia" for the first time on her American tour. Webster, who had stood to bow his approval at the end of earlier numbers, now stood and sang along with the star when she came to the chorus. Mrs. Webster pulled frantically at his coattails but the Secretary of State paid no notice, and sang accompaniment on every refrain. When the song was over, he and the songstress traded bows for curtsies at least ten times while the audience applauded.

A more poignant note was struck that evening when Lind sang "Home, Sweet Home," a largely forgotten tune written years earlier by playwright and sometime Washingtonian John Howard Payne. Payne had fallen on hard times, and Barnum arranged for him to be seated that night in the front row at the National. Lind sang the song directly to him with the full pathos of which she was capable. Payne covered his eyes, overcome with emotion.

Lind's inclusion of "Home, Sweet Home" in her repertoire vaulted it into nationwide popularity, and the song remains with us today. Payne, however, had sold his rights to the words and tune years before, and never reaped a penny from the millions of times they have since been repeated. In a last try for better fortune, he secured a posting as envoy to Tunisia. There he died only two years after his great moment with Jenny Lind at the National.

In a curious act of personal pilgrimage, W.W. Corcoran, by then vastly wealthy, traveled from Washington to Tunis to return with Payne's remains, apparently moved by a sense that the author of the famous song about home should not lie in foreign soil. On Corcoran's return, the successful songwriter and luckless businessman was reinterred in a cemetery near what is now Rock Creek Park.

Jenny Lind's two concerts reaped the staggering sum of $15,385.60. This amount would have been impossible had the singer's wishes for lower prices at the second show prevailed. She had hoped that Washington's poor could then attend, but Barnum dismissed the idea. This was Washington, he told her, and in Washington, "Everyone here is a celebrity of some kind."

THE SECOND NATIONAL

The aura of success that surrounded the Swedish Nightingale's visit to the new National Hall was not long lasting. Willard and Reeside sold the theatre and in January of 1851 it was remodeled under Manager Rufus Welch as a circus for a French equestrian troupe. The orchestra was made into a performance ring and additional tiers of seats were erected on the stage. An hour before the first show was scheduled to begin, a 30-foot-long section of six-tiered seating on the west side of the theatre crashed into the basement, "carrying at least a hundred people, ladies, gentlemen, and children down with the broken benches and rafters, a distance of sixteen feet. The confusion that ensued was indescribable. The audience rushed into the area, and escaped through the stage entrance. Active exertions were made to rescue those who were entangled in the ruins, and it was found that the only injuries received were bruises of no serious importance."

Amazingly enough, although management gave refunds to all who wished to leave, a large part of the audience elected to remain for the show. The equestrians performed on the scene of the near-disaster several times, supported by Monsieur W.F. Wallet, the "intellectual clown," who gave comic speeches on mesmerism and women's rights. Further repairs were made and a newspaper notice declared "Confidence Restored." But public confidence was not sufficiently revived to keep the theatre from closing in less than a week.

The lights came on again almost a year later in a building "strongly rebuilt and entirely remodeled," leased by E.A. Marshall, proprietor also of the Walnut Street Theatre in Philadelphia and the Broadway Theatre in New York. His opening cast drew talent from

Somewhat masculine in looks and temperament, Charlotte Cushman was America's leading native-born actress in the mid-19th century. She enjoyed playing strongly "non-feminine" woman's parts, such as Meg Merrilies, as well as male roles that included Romeo, played to her sister Susan's Juliet (above).

Iago was one of many characters Edwin Booth presented at the National in appearances over several decades. In a one-time event in New York in 1864, Edwin joined his brothers in Julius Caesar, *playing Brutus, at center, to John Wilkes's Mark Antony, at right, and Junius Brutus, Jr.'s Cassius. Despite his brother John's soon-to-come notoriety, Edwin would become the leading tragedian and later senior statesman of the American stage.*

the companies of both theatres and starred Matilda Heron, who would later create the first famous characterization of the wan courtesan Camille. Marshall's opening show on December 15, 1851 was Sheridan Knowles's *The Hunchback*. The elegant company performed before President and Mrs. Fillmore, Daniel Webster, and an array of dignitaries by now customary on opening nights. True to pattern, however, the next few nights saw talent playing to near-empty houses as the worst cold snap in 12 years kept citizens home in front of their fireplaces.

Now renamed the National Theatre, the new auditorium could seat 3,000, and had room for 1,000 more spectators in the aisles. Iron bars supported the floors and solid iron pillars held up three curving galleries beneath a domed ceiling. Heat was by steam, lights by gas; Marshall had spent $15,000 rebuilding. Box tickets were priced at $6, orchestra seats and reserved seats in the dress circle and parquet section cost 75 cents (50 cents on a first-come basis if available at show time), while the family circle, gallery, and third tier still cost a quarter.

The *Intelligencer*, always an advocate of first-rate drama with a vehement loathing of stage acts involving animals, noted with approval Marshall's "fixed purpose to keep his house uncontaminate and free from those viler uses and habitudes with which the true drama is unconnected." The editors despaired of his success after the unrewarding first week, writing, "This is the *only* place of amusement in this large city, so filled with strangers. If the present lessee fails to crowd the house, no other man in this country can flatter himself with the expectation of success. . . ."

But Marshall rebounded with a medley of stars to make the 1851–52 season a highlight of the National's early career. Before Christmas he announced the first "regular opera, with all its appointments" ever to appear in Washington (although opera stars had performed individually at the first National). Madame Celeste returned to find herself still a Washington favorite, followed by Julia Dean in the first hit written by Irish playwright and actor Dion Boucicault, *London Assurance*. The play remained one of the most popular for the rest of the century, while Boucicault revolutionized stage practice and management. Dean's Washington performances were popular enough to warrant arrangements for horsedrawn-omnibus service between Georgetown and the National before and after her shows. The fare: 12½ cents.

Dancer Lola Montez brought the allure of a scandalous reputation from European court circles to the National's stage, drawing full houses of men only. She "set the town on fire with her beauty," Hunter and Polkinhorn tell us, "and played havoc with the masculine hearts." Perhaps in a nod to feminine delicacy, newspapers ran no reviews.

Charlotte Cushman, at the height of her fame, appeared as Lady Macbeth and in other roles. Hunter and Polkinhorn relate that one evening's performance was attended by the Washington Light Infantry and the Washington Continental Guards in full uniform. After her performance the actress thanked the militias (whose functions were more social than military) with a wine supper at the nearby National Hotel.

Toward the season's end, Edwin Forrest, now uncontested as the nation's leading tragedian—Junius Brutus Booth having died of drink not long before—packed an estimated 4,000 patrons into the National on his last night, when the house's "free list" for admission was suspended—except for the press.

Marshall's managerial tenure lasted into 1854 and included the appearance of Monsieur Jullien and his orchestra before President Fillmore in November, 1853. A thousand patrons jammed the aisles in a rush for seats when the doors opened. Audience and musicians rose to their feet during a stirring medley of "American National Airs" that reached its peak with the ever-reliable crowd-pleaser, "Hail Columbia."

Themes of the nation's westward expansion were presented in a drama, the *Texas Struggle for Liberty*, and in a panoramic painting entitled *Stanley's Western Wilds*, created by the artist-explorer John M. Stanley of the Smithsonian Institute's Indian Gallery. Viewers paid half the usual prices to see the painting while appropriate music by a cornet band accompanied a lecture.

Novelty acts seem to have been less frequent than at the first National but were still common fare: The Ravels returned with their aerial feats, while Professor Anderson, the "Great Wizard of the North" gave lectures debunking witchcraft, demonology, spiritualism, and "spirit rappers" through "wonderful feats in Natural Magic and Experimental Philosophy."

The *Intelligencer* did not hide its occasional disappointment with Marshall's taste. For an unspecified breach of decorum in their act, the paper took great offense at a troupe of Chinese magicians. An occasional sparely-worded notice sniffed at groups like Mr. Donizetti's "acting monkeys, dogs, and goats," the closing draw of the 1852 season.

In spring of 1853 the paper remarked that the theatre needed sprucing up to "remove a rather frequent source of unfavorable remark from strangers visiting our city." The previous year had seen the advent of another newspaper, the *Evening Star*. It would soon usurp the *Intelligencer's* leading role, and throughout a century of publication prove to be as strong a supporter of theatre in Washington as its predecessor.

Perhaps the air of seediness noted in 1853 was the presentiment of a sinking spell that lay ahead for the National. Following Marshall's departure in 1854, George Kunkle and John T. Ford (later of Ford's Theatre) took over briefly. In January, 1855, their successor, W. Mowbray, "took his departure, on Saturday afternoon, for parts unknown, leaving unsettled numerous bills." The troupe scheduled to perform that evening hoped to go ahead with their show, but found that the gas had been turned off by the Gas Company, to whom Mowbray owed $100.

Only two days before Mowbray's disappearance, soprano Gialitto Grisi and baritone Mario commanded the highest prices yet charged at the National. The cheapest seats sold for $5 (although New York and Baltimore audiences had paid only $3, angering Washingtonians even as they paid the demanded price). Orchestra seats fetched $10, upper boxes $50, and lower boxes $75. As performances sold out, holders of tickets scalped them at astronomical prices: a Virginian who had struck it rich in the California gold rush of '49 reportedly paid a member of Congress $1,000 for his private box.

Edwin Booth's much-lauded first appearance on the National's stage in 1856 brought a hint of the overwhelming favor with which the country would soon receive the son of its deceased old favorite. Edwin's first role, earlier performed at the National by his father and later by his brother, was Richard III.

Management passed through the hands of Joseph Jefferson III and I.B. Phillips to rest, by the beginning of 1857, with Fanny Morant. The energetic manageress promised a lively season of first-rate talent, and changed the name of her new establishment to Fanny Morant's National Theatre. Mercifully the new name did not last long. On the afternoon of February 6, while preparations were underway, fire broke out in the upper part of the theatre and completely engulfed the building.

The next performance would come five years later.

ACT II:

The Golden Years

A CAPITAL AT WAR

*W*hy the National Theatre was not immediately rebuilt after the fire of 1857 is not clear. Even though the Panic of 1857 had paralyzed the economy of many American cities, the *Washington News* reported that it "prevailed to a very limited extent" in Washington, and by 1859 the *Star* observed that "the general prostration of trade" had been so brief in Washington that the city was "in a far better condition than before the blow came. There never was more hard cash in the hands of our fellow citizens than at this time." The economic stability was derived not only from the local economy, but also from the spending of the Federal government; as long as the Union prevailed, Washington's economy was stable.

The 1850s had been a time of prosperity for Washington. Population tripled from 1840 to 1860, and building lots, which had sold for four cents a square foot in 1843, were selling for 30 cents by 1854. Property values continued to rise throughout the decade. Although no structure was built on the National Theatre site during the years 1857 to 1861, Washingtonians did see construction move forward on the wings of the Capitol after the Library of Congress fire in 1851. By 1858,

Helena Modjeska, shown here as Camille, fled the Russian oppression of Poland and, in 1876, established a Polish colony in California. When that failed she turned to the stage and established herself as a star noted for her poetic and lyrical acting style.

43

A playbill advertises Cordelia Howard's Benefit Performance as Little Eva *in* Uncle Tom's Cabin. *This dramatic version of Harriet Beecher Stowe's history-making novel was written by George C. Howard, and ran for an unprecedented 100 nights in its premiere engagement in Troy, New York in 1852–53.*

Congress could move into its new halls even though the pillars of the eastern portico were not yet in place. Finally, in 1863, the Capitol dome was finished.

Perhaps the collapse of the Washington real estate market a week after the presidential election of 1860, and perhaps the problems of determining just who were the legal owners of the National Theatre property, impeded its rebuilding. After the fire of 1857 the property passed through many hands until a ruling of the Equity Court on June 13, 1858, established Davidge and Ennis as trustees. These men sold the property to W.E. Spaulding and William W. Rapley for $35,000. Rapley was a newcomer from Baltimore whose involvement signaled a sea change in the history of management at the National. Gone were the days of revolving-door actor-managers: Rapley became a respected business-man and alderman while keeping his interest in the National until his death in 1902. His son, W.H. Rapley, became treasurer of the National and later owner. The Rapleys, between father and son, would be involved with the National for the next 85 years.

Washington was a city of great contrasts during the Civil War. Abraham Lincoln arrived in Washington un-announced, unheralded, and unexpected on February 23, 1861, was inaugurated on March 4, and became a wartime President when Fort Sumter was fired upon on April 12–13. Washingtonians felt removed and se-cure from the horrors of war. On Thursday, July 16, 1861, when the troops stationed in the District marched over Long Bridge toward Manassas, Virginia, and that small creek called Bull Run, light-heartedness was the mood of the city. Parties of civilians, including some congressmen and their wives, went along to enjoy the excitement and to picnic while it was anticipated that the Union forces would quickly defeat the Confederate army. But this was not to happen; the Confederacy won the battle.

During the weekend, sounds of battle could be heard from the fighting some 20 miles away, and on Monday wounded, dying, and defeated soldiers came stream-ing into Washington. No one could describe the scene better than newspaper correspondent Walt Whitman:

The Saturday and Sunday of the battle (20th, 21st) had been parch'd and hot to an extreme—the dust, the grime and smoke, in layers, sweated in, fol-low'd by other layers again sweated in, absorb'd by those excited souls—their clothes all saturated with the clay-powder filling the air—stirr'd up everywhere on the dry roads and trodden fields by the regiments, swarming wagons, artillery, etc.—all the men with this coating of muck and sweat and rain, now recoiling back, pouring over the Long Bridge—a horrible march of twenty miles, returning to Washington baffled, humili-ated, panic-struck . . .

Grover's National Theatre, named for its manager, Leonard Grover, was also referred to as the New National, and along with Ford's Theatre led Washington's theatrical life during the Civil War. It was President Lincoln's favorite playhouse. Opened on April 22, 1862, the theatre burned on January 28, 1873. The enormous Stars and Stripes flown above it was once torn down by Confederate sympathizers, but quickly replaced by Grover, a staunch Unionist and personal acquaintance of the President. Gas jets atop the theatre spelled out VICTORY when peace was achieved.

From this moment on, until the end of the war, Washington was a city of coffins and sickbeds, its 21 hospitals holding at one time over 50,000 wounded soldiers.

Theatre in Washington responded quickly to the Civil War. At the beginning of the hostilities the small Washington Theatre at 11th and C Streets was the only major place of entertainment in the city. Built in 1822 as a public hall, it was inadequate for stage presentations, but stars such as Joseph Jefferson, E.H. Sothern and Charlotte Cushman, supported by the resident stock company, presented well-known plays. In the off-season the theatre was converted to Carusi's Dancing Saloon. Ten days after the start of the war, the *Star* announced that "The Washington Theatre has been closed for the present, the condition of affairs here just now not being favorable to theatricals." The theatre reopened after only a week, and the summer of 1861 brought overflowing houses, especially during special performances for the added session of Congress.

The success of the Washington Theatre prompted other managers to open their houses. Rapley and Spaulding erected on the site of the burned National Theatre a rather crude structure called King's Amphitheater for the purpose of holding circus performances. On November 7, 1861, an advertisement in the *Washington Star* announced that the new place of amusement would open its doors for the first time.

The prices at the amphitheater ranged from 25 cents for Social Boxes and the Colored Apartments to 50 cents for the Dress Circle and 75 cents for Orchestra Chairs. King's Amphitheater had a short life, and within five months the *Star* was announcing the opening on April 21, 1862, of the New National Theatre (also known as Grover's National Theatre in honor of Manager Leonard Grover) "built upon the most beautiful model for Dramatic and Operatic Edifices under the superintendence of Mr. Charles Getz. . . ." However, the theatre did not actually open until the next day, with a bill which consisted of Morris Barnett's *The Serious Family* and a farce, *J.J. of the War Department*, plus music by the Marine Band. Prices were raised 25 cents a ticket over those of King's National Circus.

The bill was changed for the 23rd as reported in the *Star* on April 24:

> The house was crowded in every part and the universally expressed opinion was delight in the theatre and the acting. On April 23, for the anniversary of Shakespeare's birth, a Mr. Tilton of the company recited the "Seven Ages of Man." Miss Hough, the comedienne, also sang her popular "Josiah's Courtship" which she had sung for 300 consecutive nights in New York.

Grover's National Theatre was quite different from King's Amphitheater and received much praise from the *Star:*

> Mr. W.E. Spaulding has erected the New National without regard to cost, upon the site of the old building. . . . This building as completed has the capacity for about two thousand persons. The ceilings and walls are elegantly frescoed and the boxes neatly and tastefully painted and panelled. To sum it up, Mr. Spaulding has erected the largest, most comfortable and most elegantly located theatre in the city.

The Washington theatre community continued to expand with the opening of John T. Ford's Atheneum in the remodeled 10th Street Baptist Church. When the Atheneum burned in the fall of 1862, Ford enlarged it so he could compete with Grover's National. Among several music halls, the most successful was Canterbury Hall, located on Louisiana Avenue near 6th Street, which provided a generous sampling of songs, comedy routines, circus acts, dances, and sensational melodramas. A few blocks away on 9th Street and Pennsylvania Avenue a carriage house was renovated into the Varieties Theatre, which quickly became a favorite haunt of soldiers and businessmen. Minstrel shows, musical productions, and comedies were also available at the Odd Fellow's Hall, Seaton Hall and Philharmonic Hall.

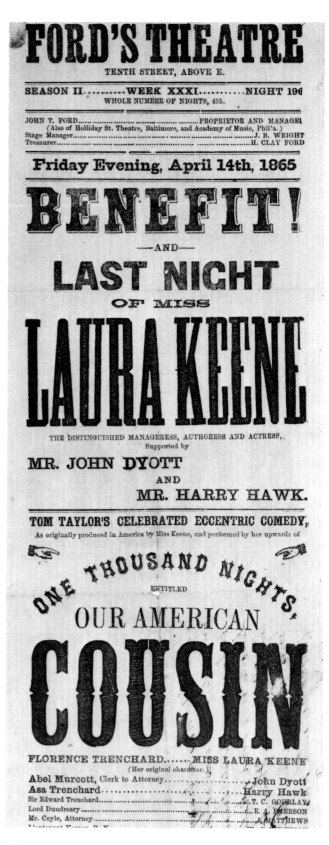

This first of the "assassination" playbills is the most famous in American theatrical history. It was being printed when word came that President Lincoln intended to visit Ford's Theatre that Friday evening. Printing was suspended and a new version drafted to include an announcement of the victory celebration and the singing of "Honor To Our Soldiers."

Favorites of audiences at these theatres were melo-dramas such as *Six Degrees of Crime*, which claimed in its advertising that it illustrated "with absorbing power, the progress toward ruin of INTEMPERANCE, LICEN-TIOUSNESS, GAMBLING, THEFT, MURDER and the SCAFFOLD." However, the theatres did respond to the war situation, and patriotic plays and topical sat-ires, although probably devoid of much artistic merit, did satisfy a need of the audiences to see more Amer-ican themes dramatized on the stage.

Grover's National and Ford's Theatre were some-what more conservative than the music halls, and in these theatres one could expect to see two short farces in addition to the main piece. Songs and dances were also interjected into the plays and included between acts. But the audiences at the theatres were hardly conservative in their behavior. Propriety prevailed in the sections reserved for ladies, but if a gentleman were forced to sit at the rear of the theatre, he was warned by the *Sunday Chronicle* that he would need an umbrella and a life preserver to protect him from the tobacco juice "which ran under his feet in a yellow sea, laden

The burden of his challenging presidency shows in Abraham Lincoln's drawn visage in a photograph taken on April 10, 1865, four days before his assassination at Ford's Theatre.

P.T. Barnum, the Great Showman, presents midgets to the Presi-dent in a political cartoon reflecting popular disillusionment with the North's string of losing generals.

· THE COMING MEN!

THE GREAT SHOWMAN—" *Mr. President, since your naval and military heroes don't seem to get on, try mine!*"
MR. LINCOLN—" *Well, I'll do it to oblige you, Friend Phineas, but I think mine are the smallest.*"

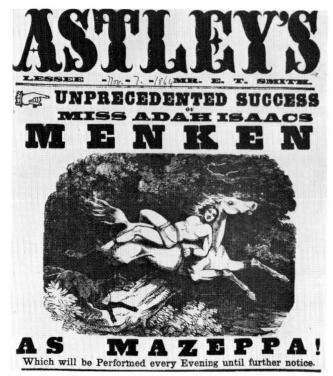

Mazeppa, or The Wild Horse of Tartary, *had originally achieved success in 1833 with Mr. Gale in the lead role. By mid-century the ''notorious'' Ada Isaacs Menken exploited this as a ''breeches role,'' appearing in flesh-colored tights and a tunic. Tod Lincoln attended* Mazeppa *at the National Theatre the night his father was assassinated.*

with peanut and chestnut shells.''

Because not all the soldiers could attend the theatres, dance halls, and variety palaces, many of them participated in their own camp theatres. On January 1, 1862, the *Star* reported that soldiers of General Auguer's brigade had erected a theatre 40 by 80 feet. On February 27, 1862, the *Star* reported that Miss Susan Denin and Benjamin Rogers were starring at a neat little theatre built by the ''men of Gen. Birney's brigade. They are assisted by volunteer 'talent,' and the 'Lyceum' flourishes amazingly. The band of the Third Maine regiment furnishes the music.''

To add to the horrors of the war, typhoid fever struck both the civilian and military inhabitants of the area. In the summer of 1862, when smallpox broke out, the President became infected. But Washington was also infected with a feverish gayety, and nurse Louisa May Alcott wrote that ''Pennsylvania Avenue, with its bustle, lights, music, and military made me feel as if I'd crossed the water and landed somewhere in Carnival time.''

Soon after the National opened in 1862, audiences there were enjoying that particular phenomenon of the 19th century American theatre called ''breeches roles,'' in which popular women stars played men's roles. Charlotte Cushman, the queen of the American theatre in the mid-1800's, drew much praise for her strong and

stirring portrayals of characters such as Romeo to her sister Susan's Juliet, and Wolsey in *Henry VIII.* In April, 1863, Susan Denin appeared as Romeo to the Juliet of Annette Ince. The notices were not good. The love scenes were considered unconvincing and Miss Denin's dueling with Tybalt was denigrated as feminine pokes suggesting a ''housemaid routing a lazy dog from a hearth rug with a broom handle.''

The year 1865 began on a spectacular note for the National. At a benefit performance for the retiring Miss Avonia Jones, John Wilkes Booth played Romeo to her Juliet. Booth's fame—or infamy—would be assured later that year at Ford's theatre. John Wilke's older brother Edwin appeared late in March with *Hamlet* as the highlight of his engagement. Shortly after, opera and more Shakespeare were presented, and for the first time at the National, *Uncle Tom and His Cabin*—undoubtedly the single most influential drama ever to play the house.

Washington was already acquainted with *Uncle Tom's Cabin,* which had been serialized in Washington's antislavery newspaper, the *National Era,* in 1851–52. Harriet Beecher Stowe's novel was first published in book form in March of 1852 and became the most widely read book of the period. C. W. Taylor quickly turned it into a play which premiered at Purdy's National Theatre in New York in August. Many other dramatizations of the novel were made and it became the most popular play of the decade preceding the Civil War. So popular was the play that the *New York Herald* feared the stage would become ''an agent for the cause of abolitionism.'' Even President Lincoln recognized the influence of *Uncle Tom's Cabin;* it has been reported that on first meeting its author, he called her ''the little lady who wrote the book that made this great war.''

For many who saw the play, the experience was not theatrical but religious, and the play brought a new audience into the theatre. Recognizing the non-theatrical nature of the *Uncle Tom and His Cabin* audience, the National Theatre's management charged a flat 30 cents for all the seats for the 1865 engagement. *Uncle Tom's Cabin* was played by travelling tent shows and cheap stock companies well into the 20th Century, but it seldom returned to the National.

LINCOLN AT THE THEATRE

The entire Washington social, political, and theatrical scene quickly changed on April 14, 1865, when President Lincoln accommodated his wife's desire to attend Ford's Theatre instead of Grover's National.

Although the National Theatre was often visited by presidents of the United States, no president has shown

A stagehand waits backstage at The Black Crook, *1866, as lightly-clad ballet girls mount a platform from which they will ''fly'' supported by wires.* The Black Crook *is often cited as the genesis of the American musical comedy.*

Lydia Thompson and her "British Blondes" brought English bur-
lesque to the American stage with popular parodies such as The
Forty Thieves *and* Sinbad. *Miss Thompson was noted for her*
perfect elocution and, this photograph notwithstanding, her
"daintiness."

Charlotte Crabtree, known as "Lotta," was one of the most popu-
lar performers on the American stage from the time of her debut
in 1867 until her retirement in 1891. Old plays were adapted to
showcase her singing, dancing, and banjo-playing, and new plays
were written specifically for her talents—which evidently included
smoking onstage.

a greater interest in theatre than Lincoln. He was a frequent visitor to Grover's National Theatre and became a close friend of the manager, Leonard Grover. Lincoln was in a private box with his host Senator Oliver Morton when John Wilkes Booth performed *Richard III* as his debut in Washington. Although John Wilkes Booth was the star of Grover's stock company, he seldom appeared in Washington, spending most of his time on tour.

According to Leonard Grover, theatre was the favorite pasttime of President Lincoln. The view is verified by Carl Sandburg in his famous Lincoln biography, in which he notes that Lincoln went to the National "perhaps a hundred times since coming to Washington."

Tad Lincoln was as much taken with the theatre as was his father, and went with him often to the National. Grover willingly loaned Tad theatrical properties and costumes which Tad used for productions in a miniature playhouse set up in the White House. Tad also managed to appear unannounced on stage at the National. Grover recounts the story, an evening in 1864 when Tad

> . . . left his father's box and went backstage and got a costume too large for him and during the number "Rally 'Round the Flag," appeared on stage in *The Seven Sisters.* . . . The President had a bad quarter of a minute of shock at the sight, but the humor of the situation quickly restored him, and he laughed immoderately.

On June 8, 1864, President Lincoln went to the National to escape the tensions of the Republican convention being held in Baltimore. Grover recounts that, about 9:00, "a messenger came from the White House with a telegram, instructed to deliver it to me. It was addressed to Mr. Lincoln; I took it to him and it was found to contain the first news for him of his nomination."

April 14, 1865, was Good Friday and the first day that the Civil War would be referred to in the past tense. In his book, *The Day Lincoln Was Shot,* Jim Bishop reconstructs the activities of that fateful day. Early in the morning Secretary of War Stanton asked his wife to send their regrets to Mrs. Lincoln; they would not be going to the theatre with the President and his wife. Stanton had urged President Lincoln on many occasions to stop attending the theatre because of the danger and to minimize all public appearances. But Stanton did not prevail.

On that same Friday morning, John Wilkes Booth left the National Hotel to meet co-conspirator George Atzerodt, who had booked a room at the Kirwood House where Vice President Johnson was staying. Atzerodt was assigned to kill the Vice President of the United States; the honor of killing the President be-

Actor John McCullough is romantically, if erroneously, said to have been murdered while playing Hamlet *at the National. Although his death elsewhere is documented, his ghost is among several reputed to haunt the theatre. In early sightings, night watchmen saw his shade trailed across the dark stage by a spectral call boy.*

Davy Crockett was a new American dramatic type, a "frontiersman without education, but with an arm of iron and a heart of gold—nature's nobleman. . . ." Frank Mayo played the role of Davy Crockett throughout his entire career.

51

longed to Booth.

At breakfast the Lincolns discussed their theatre plans for the evening. Mrs. Lincoln had tickets for the grand victory celebration at the National, but she preferred to see Laura Keene in *Our American Cousin* at Ford's. The President told Mrs. Lincoln that he expected the Grants to join them at the National for the celebration, even though it was quite clear that General Grant did not want to accept President Lincoln's invitation. Subsequently, the President acquiesced to Mrs. Lincoln and sent a request to Ford's theatre for a box, also indicating that the Grants would attend. They did not do so.

President Lincoln had experienced a premonition of his death. After seeing *Faust* on March 19, he dreamt of walking through a silent White House. In the East Room was a catafalque. "Who is dead?" he asked a guard; the reply was, "The President, he was killed by an assassin." For the next month he could not shake the dream from his thoughts. On Tuesday, April 11,

James O'Neill was enormously popular as The Count of Monte Cristo. *He was less successful in other roles, including Jesus Christ in a passion play, and was finally trapped in repeated revivals of* The Count, *which he played more than 6,000 times.*

while the city was celebrating General Lee's surrender, President Lincoln spoke of his dream again. Even earlier he had said to Harriet Beecher Stowe, author of *Uncle Tom's Cabin*, "Which ever way the war ends, I have the impression that I shall not last long after it is over."

At the Cabinet meeting on the 24th President Lincoln was compelled to bring up his dreams again, one of them from just the night before. The day continued in its ominous way. At 2:00, when the *National Intelligencer* hit the streets with the announcement that Ford's would play the farce, the "Gorgeous Play of *Aladdin or the Wonderful Lamp*" and *Our American Cousin*, the *Star* was reporting the expected appearance of General Grant with the Lincolns at the National Theatre. Bishop points out that this same afternoon, hours before the event, the Whig Press of Middleton, New York inexplicably published the news that President Lincoln had been assassinated. In Manchester, New Hampshire, people were spreading the rumor that President Lincoln was dead, while in St. Joseph, Minnesota, 40 miles away from any telegraph office, the same rumor was quickly spreading through the small community.

President Lincoln had planned to take Tad to the National to see *Mazeppa, or The Wild Horse of Tartary,*

featuring Kate Vance and her trained horse Don Juan. *Mazeppa* had been a favorite for over 30 years, and although based on Lord Byron's poem, the play provided audiences primarily with sensationalism. Miss Vance, playing the role of Mazeppa, was strapped to the back of Don Juan with her beautiful legs uncovered for all to see. As the horse sped up the precipice, higher and higher, lightning flashed, thunder rolled, a moving panorama was brought in behind her and it appeared as though Don Juan was swimming in water. At the apex of emotion and suspense, a ferocious eagle was lowered to peck at the powerless Mazeppa. The audience thrilled to the spectacle.

Tad Lincoln decided to go to the National but President and Mrs. Lincoln went to Ford's, arriving at 8:25 during the first act. Shortly after 10:00 John Wilkes Booth slipped into the President's box, and while the character Mr. Trenchard was drawling the line, "Don't know the manners of good society, eh?... Wal, I guess I know enough to turn you inside out, you sockdologizing old mantrap," Booth aimed his derringer at the back of Lincoln's head. During the laughter following Trenchard's line, he pulled the trigger.

President Lincoln's premonitions had been realized. "I'm bleeding to death," he said as the blood made a pool on the floor. At 7:22 the next morning, in an obscure boarding house across the street from the theatre, President Lincoln died. Scarcely 12 hours before, he had told his bodyguard, William Crook, that he believed there were men who wanted to take his life, and that if they were so determined, there was no way to stop them.

Tad Lincoln learned of his father's assassination in the lobby of the National Theatre as he awaited his parents' carriage which was to take him back to the White House. Grover, who was in New York at the time of the assassination, received from his associate C.D. Hess a telegram which read, "President shot tonight at Ford's Theatre. Thank God it wasn't ours."

Following the assassination, with all the theatres in Washington closing, Grover issued the following announcement:

The manager deems it proper to announce that in view of the terrible calamity which has befallen our country in the untimely death of our beloved President, he considers it meet and proper that the National shall remain closed until the general grief that overshadows our community shall have subsided. Therefore, we close the theatre indefinitely.

The city of Washington, which on Friday had been celebrating the end of the Civil War, now mourned the death of the President. Within hours the paralyzed capital became agitated by a spirit of mob revenge. Police were called to protect Ford's Theatre from crowds bent on arson. Months would pass before Washington would return to normal.

AFTER THE WAR

The National Theatre reopened in the fall of 1865 with the Holman Opera Troupe, followed a few days later by the popular light comedian, James E. Murdoch, who had just come out of retirement, then by Mrs. D.P. Bowers in the sentimental comedy, *Love's Sacrifice.* After the theatre had been repainted, Maggie Mitchell, one of the late President's favorite actresses, began a three week engagement on the 8th of January, 1866, with *Fanchon, The Cricket* and *Little Barefoot* on alternating nights. Not a bill to long remember. But the quality of the plays picked up in the latter part of March when the renowned Mr. and Mrs. Charles Kean—she was the former Miss Ellen Tree—appeared in *Henry VIII.* Capitalizing on their star drawing power, the National doubled its prices.

On June 1, John T. Ford, former owner of the ill-fated 10th Street theatre, temporarily took charge of Grover's National. He and his brother had been imprisoned for 39 days after the assassination until their innocence was established. Since Grover was no longer manager his name was dropped, and the theater was now known simply as the National Theatre again. Under Ford's management the theatre soon prospered and the best of American theater returned to the National's stage. In early December Joseph Jefferson, formerly manager, treasurer, doorkeeper, and stage manager of the National, drew crowds as Bob Acres in *The Rivals,* as the title character in *Caleb Plummer,* and in his most famous role, Rip Van Winkle.

Jefferson became immortal with his portrayal of the man who slept for years. He first became acquainted with the character when he produced Dion Boucicault's dramatization of the Washington Irving story at the Adelphi Theatre in London in 1865. When Jefferson presented his version with himself in the title role at the Olympic Theatre in New York on September 3, 1866, he created a sensation. In an editorial of December 21, 1866, the *National Intelligencer* wrote that the popularity of *Rip Van Winkle* continues "with unabated success to fill the house with an overflowing and delighted throng—a triumph never surpassed in this city." Rip Van Winkle remained in Jefferson's repertoire for 38 years until his retirement in 1904. Because he was always adjusting the role as he played it, the play was never put into final form. Jefferson's appeal was based on more than just his acting skill. As theatre historian Barnard Hewitt explains, "he was probably the most lovable man, off the stage as well as on, our theatre has known. . . ."

Next came the internationally famous Italian actress, Adelaide Ristori, who appeared in the midst of her most successful American tour, in *Marie Antoinette, Mary, Queen of Scots, Queen Elizabeth* and *Medea*. The next spring, Edwin Booth played the Cardinal in *Richelieu* for the first time in Washington.

The fall season of 1868 was highlighted with the appearance of *The Black Crook,* often cited as the first American musical. The major feature of the production was a group of ballet dancers who had been stranded in New York when the Academy of Music was destroyed by fire. Manager William Wheatly decided to incorporate them into the play, and it opened at Niblo's Garden in New York in September 1866. The resultant sensation filled the theatre for an unprecedented 18 months. Audiences were delighted with the elaborate fairyland scenery, but probably even more so with the women who wore scanty costumes that showed off their legs.

Although the National was prospering greatly and attracting the most famous of American and foreign stars, it had fallen into disrepair. In his 1869 guidebook, *Sights and Sounds of the Nation's Capital,* John Ellis wrote that both the National and Wall's Opera House were dirty and old-fashioned and that "they would rank as second-class establishments in other cities, and contrast strangely with the audiences which they sometimes contain." Ellis did not think much of the acting either; to him, the only good acting came from the travelling troupes, and "actors who could not earn a decent living in our larger cities flourish in Washington and furnish food for the dramatic criticisms of the grave and reverend seigneurs of the Government.' "

Obviously the condition of the theatre did not improve, for the next year one John Montgomery Gordon wrote to the Mayor and City Council complaining about conditions at the National and Wall's. He was especially concerned about fire hazards such as chairs in the narrow aisles, uncovered flame in the footlights, dangerous lamps in the audience, and flammable scenery. Gordon's concern for fire hazards at the National was well founded, for on January 28, 1873, at 11:00 in the morning, fire destroyed much of the theatre and most of the scenery of the Alice Oates Opera Company. William Rapley, the co-owner, arrived at the theatre just before the fire started, but could do nothing to stop the blaze. Valued at $138,000, the theatre was covered by only $98,000 worth of insurance. Rapley bought out Mr. Spaulding and began to rebuild immediately.

While the National Theatre was being rebuilt, the city of Washington was in financial peril. Just two years

Joseph Jefferson, III showed great versatility in Rip Van Winkle, *playing both the young and the old Rip. One of the most loved of American actors, Jefferson became synonymous with* Rip, *playing the role more than 2500 times over a 38-year period. He presented* Rip *often in the city where his stage career had begun. A 1903 National booking came near the end of his almost 70 years of intermittent association with the playhouse.*

NEW NATIONAL THEATRE

TELEPHONE MAIN 501.

WM. H. RAPLEY, - - - - - - - - Manager
WM. H. FOWLER, - - - - - - - - Treasurer

WEEK OF MONDAY, NOVEMBER 16, 1903.

MONDAY, TUESDAY, THURSDAY NIGHTS, AND SATURDAY MATINEE.

JOSEPH JEFFERSON
IN
"RIP VAN WINKLE"

CAST OF CHARACTERS.

ACT I.

Rip Van Winkle	Joseph Jefferson
Derrick Von Beekman	John Jack
Cockles (His Nephew)	W. W. Jefferson
Nick Vedder	Percy Plunkett
Jacob Stine	Charles Duval
Clausen	D. Jones
Little Heindrich	Ipha Yenair
Little Meenie	Dolly Oweise
Gretchen	Ffolliott Paget

ACT II.

Rip Van Winkle	Joseph Jefferson
Gretchen	Ffolliott Paget
Little Heindrich	Ipha Yenair
Little Meenie	Dolly Oweise

ACT III.

Rip Van Winkle	Joseph Jefferson
Dwarf	Dudley McCann
Heindrich Hudson	Robert Brown

ACTS IV AND V.

Rip Van Winkle	Joseph Jefferson
Derrick Von Beekman	John Jack
Cockles (His Nephew)	W. W. Jefferson
Heindrich Vedder (Nick Vedder's Son)	Joseph Jefferson, Jr.
Seth	Harry Odlin
Gretchen	Ffolliott Paget
Meenie	Blanche Bender
Katchen	Meta Greene

SYNOPSIS OF SCENES.

ACT I—Village of Falling Water.
ACT II—Rip's Home.
ACT III—Catskill Mountains.
ACT IV—Village of Falling Water. (An elapse of 20 years.)
ACT V—Derrick Von Beekman's Home.
Intermission of two minutes between Acts IV and V.

(Continued on Page 15.)

earlier, Congress had created the Territory of the District of Columbia from areas known as Washington, Georgetown and Washington County. Named by President Grant to the Board of Public Works as vice president, Alexander Robey Shepherd led the Board into a spending spree that within two years bankrupted the District Government. By September, 1873, the failure of the banking house of Jay Cooke & Company precipitated a nationwide depression. In Washington, the salaries of school teachers, policemen, firemen, and other employees could not be paid, and city residents found it impossible to meet their taxes. Remarkably, construction of the new National Theatre was not affected. Rapley, now sole owner, still believed that a theatre audience existed in destitute Washington. Among regular habitues of his playhouse were Alexander "Boss Shepherd," President Grant, and General William Tecumseh Sherman.

The National Theatre reopened on December 1, 1873, with apparently few major changes from the previous structure. The *Star* reported that the opening night, with President Grant in attendance, "was a very brilliant spectacle. The decorations of the house are exceedingly neat and tasteful, the colors harmonize well, the light is good, and when the sets are filled with a fashionable audience such as that of last night, the effect is quite fine."

THE FOURTH NATIONAL

The highlight of the season was the appearance of Frank Mayo in Frank Murdoch's *Davy Crockett*. Mayo and Murdoch were introducing a new American dramatic type to the stage, a "frontiersman without education, but with an arm of iron and a heart of gold—nature's nobleman . . ." The play is melodrama at its best. Davy and his new love, Eleanor, are in his backwoods hut reading poetry when wolves surround the hut, wanting to devour those inside. Davy rushes to secure the door, but the latch-bar has burnt up. Davy replaces it with his strong right arm. The howling wolves hurl themselves against the door, but Davy stands for hours, strong and stalwart. Help arrives and Davy's arm, swollen and bleeding, is extricated. With nary a moment of rest, Davy starts to walk 10 miles to the nearest settlement for additional help.

What red-blooded American could resist such heroism? The conflict between America and England, which had been the basis for many American plays, was now replaced with the conflict between Western

W.H. Rapley succeeded his father, W.W. Rapley, as owner of the National. Between them they were involved in its ownership and management for more than 85 years.

Bargain prices are advertised below an electric sign at the turn-of-the-century National, where a group of boy visitors poses on a summer day.

strength and goodness and Eastern corruption and weakness. As Joseph Jefferson did with Rip Van Winkle, Mayo continued to play Davy Crockett for the rest of his career.

Later in the season the great Italian actor, Tommaso Salvini, played at the National on his first American tour in *Ingomar*. Noted for his incredibly muscular physique, tremendous emotional intensity, and magnificent voice, Salvini later made Othello his signature role. On this first tour Salvini brought with him an Italian-speaking cast; on his subsequent four tours, he hired American actors for his company, thus producing a bilingual production.

The foreign visiting celebrities continued to provide the greatest share of theatrical excitement for Washington audiences. The Polish star Mme. Janauschek opened the fall, 1874 season with Schiller's *Mary Stuart*, followed within two weeks by the highly praised British actress Adelaide Neilson, who was revered as

A new curtain painted in 1890 by E.A. Morange presented an allegory of spring, depicting two classical deities in a chariot drawn by a team of two birds in flight, framed in voluminous painted draperies. As the chariot crosses the sky, the goddesses strew petals to the earth.

Ben Hur toured the United States after its 1899 New York opening until replaced by movie versions. It afforded one of the most lavish spectacles ever presented at the National Theatre. In the 1905 production were 350 actors and eight horses. When *Ben Hur* returned in 1910, the cast had shrunk to 200, but the number of horses had increased to 20.

Shakespeare's Viola and Juliet.

Again in the summer of 1875 John Ford took control of the National, opening the fall season with the Irish-born John McCullough, who appeared with limited success in *Hamlet*. McCullough had arrived from Ireland at the age of 15, destitute, illiterate and unable to write his name. Muscular, possessing a voice of great power and range and exhibiting the kind of animal magnetism that had made Edwin Forrest an American idol, McCullough was hired by Forrest to play supporting roles. After five years with Forrest, McCullough's acting style became so similar to that of Forrest that the star urged him to change for the sake of his career and progress as an artist. McCullough took the advice and developed in his own right into an actor of considerable ability and public appeal, appearing to his best advantage in such plays as *Virginius, Brutus, Damon and Pythias, Julius Caesar* and *The Gladiator*.

Although McCullough's Hamlet was not especially noteworthy, it is the basis for the apocryphal story that McCullough died at the National while performing Hamlet, and that his ghost still haunts the theatre. The myth is that McCullough was murdered backstage and

that fellow actors buried him in the dirt under the stage rather than let his body be consigned to a pauper's grave. Night watchmen have claimed through the years that McCullough's ghost roams the theatre on the eve of new productions, inspecting the scenery to be sure that all is ready for the opening night audience. As late as October, 1896, the ghost in the garb of Hamlet was reported as turning up at the prompter's table.

But alas, there is no foundation for the tale. After suffering a physical and mental collapse at McVicker's Theatre in Chicago on September 29, 1884, McCullough was confined in the Bloomingdale Sanitarium in New York for four months and then moved to his home in Philadelphia. There he died on November 8, 1885, of paresis, the result of congenital syphillis. Yet who knows? Perhaps McCullough's ghost does return to the National Theatre, which he often referred to as his favorite playhouse.

The possibility of fire in 19th-Century theatres was always real and always provided the potential for catastrophe. A panic was narrowly averted on Christmas night of 1876, when Kate Claxton was performing in the ever-popular melodrama, *The Two Orphans*. During the snow scene, a fight that broke out in the balcony caused a general disturbance in the theatre. Such fights were not uncommon during the period, but the disturbance increased and soon calls of "Fight!" "Fight!" changed to "Fire!" "Fire!" and the audience began to panic.

Many in the audience were not surprised that something untoward would happen while Miss Claxton was performing at the National. She was gaining the reputation of being followed by a dark cloud; it seemed that catastrophe occurred wherever she appeared. Several months earlier, while she was playing the title role in *Louise* in Brooklyn, a fire broke out that gutted the theatre and took 200 lives. Remembering Kate's recent fire in New York and the National's history of conflagration, the Washington audience rushed to the exits. Cool-headed ushers quickly threw open the doors so there would be no pile-up. The orchestra played a lively tune, peace was restored, and after a brief delay, *The Two Orphans* continued in its tale of woe and despair.

The fall season of 1877 was highlighted by Lydia Thompson and her British Blondes. Thompson and her company had caused a sensation in New York in 1869 when they introduced British burlesque to the American stage with their production of *Sinbad*. The appearance in Washington of beautiful blondes in scanty costumes caused outcries against "nudity" on stage, but such attacks from pulpits and newspapers only increased the magnitude of the company's box office appeal. At the National, audiences flocked to see Miss Thompson as Robinson Crusoe, with her company of women playing pirates in silk tights. What the audience experienced was well-spoken English, parodies of well-known literature, dancing, songs, ditties, jokes, and

Advertisements in National Theatre programs modishly reflect life of the early 20th century.

Maude Adams was loved as much for her personal goodness and wholesomeness as for her acting ability. She is best remembered for her portrayal of Peter Pan in J.M. Barrie's Peter Pan, The Boy Who Wouldn't Grow Up. *At the peak of her career she was the top money-making star in the country.*

the continuation of the "breeches" tradition. That same season John McCullough played his repertoire of tragic roles, and Joseph Jefferson returned for yet another successful run of *Rip Van Winkle.*

The year 1878 began on a high note with the appearance of the renowned Lawrence Barrett in *Richelieu* and *Hamlet.* That spring Polish star Mme. Helen Modjeska made her National debut in *Camille.* Mme. Modjeska had fled political persecution in Poland and had come to the United States, where she built a distinguished artistic reputation. Dion Boucicault, John McCullough, and Lotta Crabtree followed later in the year.

In September, 1878, the management of the National Theatre came into new hands, although Rapley remained the owner. John T. Albaugh of the Holliday Street Theatre in Baltimore became the new lessee and manager. During his first season he presented, among others, William F. Cody, better known as Buffalo Bill, in a "blood and thunder" piece called *Lost and Found.* Later came the first presentation at the National of Shakespeare's *King John,* with F.C. Bangs. The fall, 1878 season featured such stars as Lotta, Mme. Modjeska, Lawrence Barrett and Joseph Jefferson, and during the Christmas holidays, the lighter fare of Haverley's Horse Opera.

The new Gilbert and Sullivan opera, *H.M.S. Pinafore,* opened at the National on April 16, 1879, after a phenomenal run of 100 nights in New York. The production was received enthusiastically by audiences and critics alike, as witnessed by a local reviewer who wrote that *Pinafore* was music "that people could understand; the music sparkled, laughed, flashed. It was opera by the people, for the people and of the people, and they claimed and adopted *Pinafore* as theirs." So popular was this new opera that shortly after the Washington run, a black version of *Pinafore* played the National, and in the fall, Haverly's Chicago Church Choir Company appeared with its version.

The early 1880s continued the pattern established in the late 1870s of presentations with an emphasis upon musical entertainment, melodramas, comedies, and the appearance of stars in their most popular roles. Productions such as *Camille, Aida, Carmen, Lohengrin, The Black Crook, Davy Crockett* and Gilbert and Sullivan's

The Pirates of Penzance, and stars such as John McCullough, Mary Anderson, Joseph Jefferson, Lawrence Barrett, Henry Irving, Ellen Terry, and Helen Modjeska were regular visitors.

During the period of 1881–1885 there were two events of great significance. The first was the debut in Washington on April 8, 1881, of Sarah Bernhardt. She opened as Gilberte in *Frou Frou,* a characterization in which William Winter praised her as "a perfect image of winning prettiness, unconscious coquetry and exquisite, if irrational sensibility, a passionate woman and . . . a fascinating child." The public was as taken with the "Divine Sarah" as was Winter. Her performance is described in the *Washington Star:*

> The audience last night at the National Theatre, despite the treble prices, was not only immense, but of the highest quality, almost everyone of prominence in society, of public and professional life was there. Many were there who had not been in a theatre for years. Madame Bernhardt won more and more upon her audience, and she was called out by the wildly enthusiastic audience again and again.

The second major event was the revival by Lawrence Barrett of George Henry Boker's *Francesca Da Rimini* in early 1883. Historian Barnard Hewitt credits this play "as the best written in America before the present century. It is clearly the finest fruit of the romantic drama in America . . . " However, the play was not a success when first produced in 1855 by Edward L. Davenport. Barrett's fine performance renewed interest in the play and for the next two decades *Francesca da Rimini* was frequently revived. Barrett returned with his hit in the spring and was followed by the Washington premiere of James O'Neill in *The Count of Monte Cristo,* a role O'Neill was to perform more than 6,000 times during the next 30 years. Although O'Neill tried other roles, his adoring public forced him to return again and again to the Count. The bitterness he felt and his resentment at having been successful only as a one-role actor are the basis for much of the play, *Long Day's Journey Into Night,* written by his son, Eugene.

The 1884–85 season promised a series of crowd pleasers. Opening with traditional minstrels, the National next presented Frank Mayo, Mme. Janauschek, Joseph Jefferson, Mlle. Rhea—a French actress of much popularity—the exceptional Madison Square Repertory Company from New York, Fanny Davenport, and a host of other well-known performers. William Rapley and Samuel Kingsley, now jointly managing the theatre, anticipated an exceptionally profitable season. But such was not to be, for on February 27, 1885, three hours after Wallack's New York Company completed its performance of *Victor Durand,* fire broke out. By 2:30 a.m. the rear wall fell in, followed half an hour later

Sarah Bernhardt, who never did anything halfway, expressed her regard for a Washington establishment with a note translated as follows:

> Mr. Achille Burklin:
>   *I can say, without hesitation, that you are the best and most wonderful dyer and cleaner I have ever known. Your work surpasses that of all cleaners of all countries, including even those of my own beautiful France.*
>
> With my warmest regards,
Sarah Bernhardt, Paris

"The Divine Sarah" Bernhardt toured the United States many times between 1880 and 1917, performing an astonishing array of roles. She was especially revered by audiences for her performance in the 19th-century domestic melodrama, Camille.

by the collapse of the front wall. The loss was estimated at $150,000, but less than a quarter of that amount was covered by insurance. Also destroyed in the fire were the Miller and Jones Billiard Parlor over the lobby and the sample rooms for a firm located on the west side of the lobby. For the fourth time in fifty years, the National Theatre lay in smouldering ruins.

THE FIFTH NATIONAL

Within two months, reconstruction of the National Theatre began, and by October of 1885 the building was ready for use. Although the structure was completed in September, five more weeks were needed to ready the 1900-seat interior. The 1873 building had been a two-story eclectic structure with nine tall windows across its upper story and a cornice with balustrade above. The 1885 structure was five stories high of Italianate style and remained basically unaltered until 1922. The change from the simple to the more elaborate theatre reflected the more cosmopolitan tastes of the growing metropolis called Washington, D.C.

The interior had been vastly improved from its predecessor's. Because the New National (as it was now called) was lit by electricity, the hundred-burner chandelier in the auditorium was converted from gas; an asbestos fireproof curtain separating the stage from the auditorium was installed; the seats were larger and more comfortable; the orchestra and the green room were heavily carpeted; and twenty-four dressing rooms were provided. The building was heated by steam.

The New National Theatre opened on October 5, 1885, with Mlle. Rhea in *Lady Ashley.* Praise was given by the *Star* the next day for the beautiful curtain. At the end of the second act the audience called long and loudly for Manager Rapley, but he was too shy to appear on stage, and Dr. Frank Howe made a speech of thanks for him.

The curtain which had received such praise on opening night lasted only five years. In 1890 the artist E.A. Morange was commissioned to design and execute a new curtain depicting an allegory of spring, consisting of two classical women in a chariot drawn by a team of birds in flight amid voluminous drapes. As the chariot crosses the sky, the two women strew petals to the earth.

By 1885 theatre was big business in the United States and flourished in all the cities throughout the nation. Individual theatres could not maintain full acting companies so they booked traveling repertory companies or individual productions from New York. To handle the requests for attractions, booking agencies grew up in New York and sent troupes to tour all over the country.

For several years after the opening of the New National in 1885, the theatre was a major house for New York shows, especially those which featured music and could boast a well-known star. Occasionally the pattern varied. Of significance was the scheduling by Richard Mansfield, during his engagement in late November, 1889, of two special matinees on Wednesday and Saturday, November 27 and 30. They were announced in the playbill of the previous week in the following manner:

An unusually interesting and notable feature of Mr. Mansfield's engagement will be the performance of Ibsen's social drama *A Doll's House*. The famous Norwegian has many admirers in Washington who will gladly avail themselves of this opportunity of seeing one of the famous writer's plays on stage in English. Art critics in London have developed a perfect craze for Ibsen's curious dramas, and the production of *A Doll's House* created a positive sensation recently in Boston and Philadelphia.

A Doll's House may have been a success in Boston and Philadelphia but it was not wildly popular in New York—even though in 1883 Helena Modjeska produced a version which had a happy ending! It died quickly. As late as 1894, William Winter in the *New York Tribune* was pronouncing Ibsen's plays "unpleasant," "obnoxious," "odiferous," "a horrible mess," "dull and dirty," and predicting that they would never prosper in the United States and that "the health and good sense of the American audience will never accept the nauseous offal of Mr. Ibsen's dissecting table as either literature or drama." The 1889 Washington production was not reviewed. Noted for his independence and courage in producing out-of-the-ordinary plays, Mansfield took his Washington production to New York where it was attacked by the critics. The two matinees were so disastrous that New York theatre historian George Odell claimed that the second matinee "ended the 'new' movement in the drama as far as English-speaking performances were concerned." Both Odell and Winter were wrong, and Ibsen was to become a world-acclaimed playwright.

The New National enjoyed a good reputation in the 1890's as evidenced by Robert Smiley's description in his "The Night Side of Washington," praising the theatre as "presenting high class drama and opera." Performances were given at 8:00 every night, except Sunday, with a matinee on Saturday. The price of admission ranged from 25 cents to $1.50, and the regular season was supplemented by a summer season of standard comedies presented over ten weeks by the National Stock Company.

Washingtonians could look with some pride on their city as it moved into the 20th Century. Writing in the *Atlantic Monthly*, A. Maurice Low praised the city for the honesty, efficiency and economy of its public

ZIEGFELD'S FOLLIES

Dazzling presentations masterminded by Florenz Ziegfeld brought glamour and laughter to Washington. Dedicated to "Glorifying the American Girl," annual editions of *The Ziegfeld Follies* included comedians, vaudeville turns, lavish scenery, and exquisitely gowned women in extravagantly staged spectacles. Ziegfeld's vision of the statuesque and buxom charmer influenced Hollywood, where many of his beauties and comics enlarged their fame.

Ziegfeld's wife, Anna Held, allegedly pampered her delicate ivory skin with daily milk baths, and acquired her wasp waist through surgical removal of her lowermost ribs. Ziegfeld starred his archetypal Venus first with "The Anna Held Girls," and later in his Follies, which she reputedly inspired.

The homespun humor of the beloved cowboy-satirist, Will Rogers, often lampooned bureaucratic bumbling and federal foibles.

Ed Wynn was one of the deft and daffy comics who mugged their way to glory in Ziegfeld shows.

Among the celebrated charms of diminutive but much-admired Ann Pennington were counted her dimpled knees.

Droll farceur W.C. Fields juggled and told jokes for Ziegfeld and became a legendary cinema wit.

Irrepressible zany Fanny Brice delighted audiences with her rollicking comic characterizations.

A true pioneer of the American theatre, Mrs. Minnie Maddern Fiske helped to introduce the more realistic style of acting to the American stage. Among Mrs. Minnie Maddern Fiske's greatest contributions to the maturation of American theatre was her championing of the plays of Henrik Ibsen. She excelled as Hedda Gabler, a role which allowed her to exhibit her natural, simple style of acting based on psychological truthfulness.

administration, the courtesy shown by the police, the city's low taxes, model schools, splendid care of public health and protection of the indigent and poor. Washington's government had come a long way from the irregularities of 1873. Living conditions at the turn of the century were not uncomfortable. As Constance Green points out in her book, *Washington Capital City, 1879–1950*, the widows of generals and statesmen ran many of the most select boarding houses, where for the high sum of $5.00 a resident could receive good food and the privilege of being introduced into proper etiquette at the dinner table.

INTO A NEW CENTURY

By 1900 the social scene in Washington was changing and no longer did a Southern background weigh heavily in one's social position. When the Social Register first appeared in 1900, few included could claim third-generation status. Washington was still a city of relative newcomers, except that Georgetowners felt superior to other Washingtonians because of their "sense of dignified antiquity."

The artistic and creative life of Washington was burgeoning with sculpture scattered throughout the city, in buildings, in squares and circles, in public areas and in such newly opened museums as the Corcoran Gallery. Commissions were formed to improve the city, and when Theodore Roosevelt was sworn in as President after the assassination of President McKinley in September of 1901, the city quickly responded to the new President's sense of idealism, determining to make Washington a model for the rest of the country.

Besides the New National, other theatres that Washingtonians could frequent were Willard Hall, soon to be razed for an addition to the Willard Hotel; Albaugh's Opera House at 15th and E Streets; the Manassas Panorama, 15th and E Streets; the Belasco Theatre at 17 Madison Place; the Dumbarton Theatre on Wisconsin Avenue; and the soon-to-be-built Shubert Theatre on 9th Street.

The early 20th Century saw important New York pro-

ducers and foreign luminaries include the New National as a major stop on their theatrical circuit. Sir Henry Irving, the first English actor to be knighted, appeared in January, 1904, with a spectacular production of Sardou's *Dante*. In four acts and twelve scenes, it purported to give a picture of several incidents in Dante's life. Forty speaking parts did not seem to impress a local reviewer, who wrote that "despite the fine performances of the star and the company, the presentation is noted for its scenic rather than its poetic and dramatic quality."

A future knight of the British Empire had preceded Sir Henry on the National's stage. On December 14, 1900, young Winston Churchill, fresh from his exploits in the Boer War, lectured on "The War As I Saw It."

In late January, 1904, Charles Frohman, "the Star Maker," presented for the first time in Washington a quiet, unassuming, religious young lady who was to become one of the most beloved actresses in the American theatre, in a dramatic trifle only made palatable

While the nation was sinking into the depths of the Depression, The Green Pastures, *based on the Bible and profoundly religious in spirit, but homey and humorous, became one of the theatre's biggest hits. God is portrayed as a black preacher, and Gabriel is an amiable giant ready to carry out the orders of "De Lawd."*

A music professor at Howard University in Washington, D.C., Todd Duncan, gained fame as Porgy in Gershwin's Porgy and Bess. *He was also instrumental in the struggle to allow blacks to attend the National Theatre.*

by her performance. Maude Adams triumphed in the role of Pepita in *The Pretty Sister of José*, a part that gave her the opportunity to sing a Spanish song. But the great adulation Miss Adams was to experience would not come until 1905, when she returned for her premiere performance in Washington of James M. Barrie's *Peter Pan*. Although she had gained stardom with the role of Babbie in Barrie's *The Little Minister*, her name would be forever linked with the role of Peter Pan. Even though Washington critics did not consider the role one of her greatest, audiences took Miss Adams to their hearts, and her place in American theatre was assured with *Peter Pan*.

The New National was a favorite for musical productions in the early 1900s. In March of 1904, the Metropolitan Opera brought *Faust*, *The Barber of Seville*, and *Carmen*. They played to standing room only and hundreds were turned away at the theatre. John Philip Sousa and his band performed on April 11, and two weeks later Richard Strauss appeared with his wife Pauline in the final performances of their American tour. Not until 1921 would they tour again.

In November Mme. Nellie Melba, remembered for the dessert bearing her name, appeared in concert after her triumphant engagement in Europe. Early the next year Mme. Ernestine Schumann-Heink from the Met played her first engagement in Washington. It was followed by the first English performance in Washington of Wagner's *Parsifal*. The production had been modeled on that at Bayreuth, and the extensive scenery required 46 baggage cars to transport it. Two singers were employed in each principal role. The performance began at 5:30, a dinner intermission lasted from 7:15 to 8:30, and the curtain came down at 10:40. It was the most ambitious operatic work ever seen in Washington.

But elaborate productions were not rare on the New National's stage. Four months after *Parsifal* had taxed the capabilities of the theatre, and after triumphant productions of Shakespeare by E.H. Sothern and Julia Marlowe and equally successful appearances by William Gillette and Maude Adams, the ultimate theatrical spectacle took over the theatre. On April 29, 1905, producers Klaw and Erlanger announced their "Stupendous Production of Gen. Lew Wallace's Mighty Play, *Ben-Hur*, Staged on a scale of unparalleled Splendor."

Three hundred and fifty persons were in the cast and eight horses were used for the "thrilling chariot-race scene."

Klaw and Erlanger returned five years later with a new production of *Ben-Hur* in seven acts and a prologue. This time there were only 200 persons in the cast, but the number of horses increased to 20. It was highly praised as "wonderfully realistic" and played to excited audiences for a full week.

The two producers also chose the New National for the premiere of yet another of their stupendous spectacles, *Kismet*, with Otis Skinner as Hajj, the beggar. The theatre was closed on December 18 and 19 of 1911 for remodeling of the stage necessary to accommodate four carloads of massive scenery. Forty feet of the stage was replaced and a trap was set in the floor to contain the tank used as a bathing pool in the exotic harem scenes. The theatre's lighting capacity was more than tripled. All the ropes and pins used in the suspension system were replaced, a property room was added to the west side of the stage house, and additional dressing rooms were built beneath the stage to accommodate the 130-member cast. Even the lobby of the theatre was

Washington, D.C.'s own Helen Hayes proved her extraordinary versatility in Victoria Regina *with Vincent Price. Within the play, Miss Hayes's remarkable range took her Victoria from 18-year-old to aging queen.*

refurbished as an Arabian tent to match the onstage atmosphere. After this national premiere in Washington, *Kismet* played continuously in various parts of the country for the next three years.

The *Ziegfeld Follies* had always enjoyed success in its visits to the New National, and so it was with some surprise that the *Ziegfeld Follies of 1912* encountered opposition. The Aloysius Truth Society, a Roman Catholic organization headed by the Rev. August J. Duertie, protested the production, and gained from Major Sylvester of the police department assurance that there would be an official censor at the theatre on opening night, February 26, 1912, a practice that was followed by the police whenever there was concern about the propriety of a production.

The Truth Society was convinced that the public morality was endangered by "a rampage of song, dance, beauty, high kicking, and other such acts." What the group objected to most and demanded be removed from the production was the "disgraceful" scene called "New Year's Eve on the Barbary Coast," a ballet depicting "a wild evening with a turkey trot on San Francisco's Barbary coast." The protest only helped busi-

ness, and despite one of the worst rainstorms of the season, the New National was overflowing, with five rows of standees at the back of the auditorium. The "disgraceful" scene in question, Act I, Scene IV, was enthusiastically received and the policemen in the audience did not ring down the curtain. Julia Murdoc of the *Washington Times* wrote on February 27, 1912 that the disputed scene was "childishly innocent."

The *Ziegfeld Follies* continued their successful runs at the New National and long lines greeted the first day of sales when the box office opened on November 17 for the 1918 edition. In this 12th annual version were songs by Irving Berlin, and the cast included W.C. Fields, Eddie Cantor, Marilynn Miller, and Will Rogers. Conscious of the war, the producers announced in the program that "The male members of this company have either served with the colors, are exempted or are ineligible for military service."

Censorship became an issue again on June 12, 1934, when Washington's assistant district attorneys recommended that the Robertson and Nicholson comedy, *Sailor, Beware!*, be closed. However, District Attorney Leslie Garnett attended the summer-stock production and found the show "a little suggestive" but not obscene. For this second week of its run the show had been cleaned up, and the censorship squad of the Women's Bureau of the Metropolitan Police Department also found the play acceptable. As earlier, two uniformed police officers sat in the audience with a stop-order to enforce if they received the signal from the district attorney who was watching the production. Members of the press thought the whole affair a publicity stunt.

The charge of obscenity was leveled by the Women's Bureau against James Kirkland's *Tobacco Road* when it opened at the National in April, 1936. However, seven assistant district attorneys disagreed, and when it was determined that the play had been considerably cleaned up for its Washington opening, the theatre manager, Steve Cochran, was not prosecuted. Between 1936 and 1942, *Tobacco Road* played the National eight times, always to good houses. As critic Bernie Harrison of the *Washington Times-Herald* wrote, "the more we pan, the more money the show makes."

On February 11, 1945, the district attorney ordered the "church rape scene" deleted from *Dark of the Moon,* and in October, some lines and one entire scene were deleted from Robert E. Sherwood's *The Rugged Path* for a performance attended by President and Mrs. Harry S. Truman, who invited the cast to the White House for dinner after the show.

Even though the movies were becoming very popular in the 1920s, the New National continued to prosper. But W.H. Rapley realized that the theatre was now inadequate to properly handle the large shows coming out of New York. In 1922 the newest version of the National was 37 years old and becoming outmoded.

71

Lillian Gish gained fame for her performance in D.W. Griffith's "The Birth of a Nation" in 1915, but interrupted her many screen performances with appearances on the legitimate stage. A 1937 hit at the National was Hamlet, *starring Miss Gish as Ophelia and John Gielgud as the Dane.*

Rapley decided to completely renovate the building, tearing down and rebuilding major portions of the structure built by his father.

Rachel Crother's *Nice People,* which a year earlier had opened New York's Klaw Theatre, now closed the New National. After the curtain fell, the orchestra played "Auld Lang Syne." The curtain rose once more and the audience sat silently as stagehands removed all the scenery, a moment described by the *Washington Post* as "a unique ceremony in the history of the theatre."

The threat of censorship occasionally threatened productions at the National. When Dark of the Moon *played the theatre in February, 1945, with Carol Stone and Richard Hart, the District Attorney ordered that the "church rape scene" be deleted.*

The strict child labor laws of the District of Columbia caused problems for producers who brought plays with children's roles to Washington. When the popular Life With Father *came to the National in 1944, the role of Harlan Day had to be written out of the script before the play could be presented.*

THE SIXTH NATIONAL

After the closing in the spring of 1922, the sixth theatre building opened that same year. The word "New" was dropped by Rapley and the playhouse was once again called the National Theatre. Because of the tragedy that January, in which an extremely heavy accumulation of snow had collapsed the Knickerbocker Theatre's roof, killing and injuring many patrons, all Washington theatres were ordered by the city Commissioners to reinforce their roofs with steel beams. In order not to disturb the National's fine acoustics, the beams were added to the outside of the structure.

Inside the auditorium, columns that had caused sight problems were replaced by a 30-ton steel girder supporting the weight of the tiers. The 12 enclosed boxes on the sides of the theatre were replaced by boxes suspended from the walls. The orchestra pit was enlarged, extending it three feet under the stage, and the lighting booth which had jutted out into the gallery was set into the rear wall.

Construction did not proceed as rapidly as expected and was not finished when the National opened again on November 27, 1922, with the melodrama *Bull Dog Drummond*. The interior decorations had not been finished but the program announced that everything would be completed by the summer of 1923. At this time the National was facing competition from both legitimate houses and the motion picture theatres. Among Washington's most popular theatres were the Belasco, the Columbia, the Garrick, Poli's, the Academy of Music, Albaugh's Grand Opera House, the President, the Avenue Grand, the Gayety, the Dumbarton, the Savoy, The Knickerbocker and the Metropolitan theatres.

Although Freemont Rider in his guidebook, *Rider's Washington*, commented in 1924 that the National was "no longer Washington's leading playhouse," the theatre continued to attract large audiences to its popular New York hits. It did not escape the turmoil that accompanied the growth of unionism, a dominant feature of the 1920's. Relations between the theatre and the various unions had been harmonious for years, but when the National Theatre Stock Company, specifically organized for summer activity, found that it could not afford to hire the regulation seven-man orchestra demanded by the musician's union, and when negotiations for a smaller orchestra fell through, the theatre cut short its 1929 summer season.

The early 1930s saw William Gillette in his signature piece, *Sherlock Holmes,* and Fred and Adele Astaire performing in *The Band Wagon* in February of 1932. The next month Lynn Fontanne brought in Eugene O'Neill's *Strange Interlude,* complete with the dinner intermission. But more problems with the musicians' union imperiled the opening of the 1932 summer season, threatening the jobs of 50 to 60 persons at a time

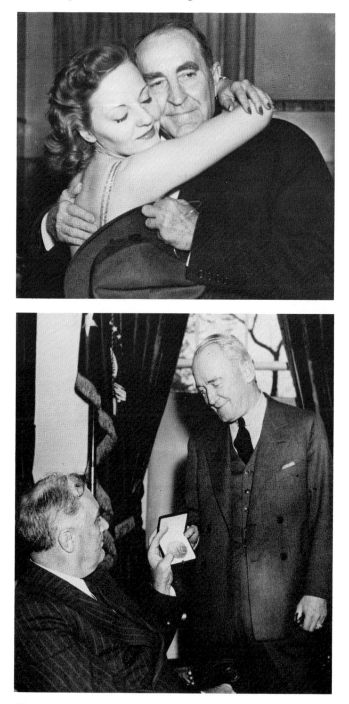

Tallulah Bankhead was a favorite of Washington audiences when she appeared in George Kelly's Reflected Glory *in 1937, and a favorite too of her father, Democratic Congressman William B. Bankhead from Alabama, Speaker of the House of Representatives. The Speaker was so proud of her that when she appeared at the National, he would "buy out the entire orchestra and invite the whole Congress to come see his daughter."*

The National Theatre was crowded for the George M. Cohan production of I'd Rather Be Right. *Cohan received enthusiastic praise for his portrayal of President Franklin Delano Roosevelt. On May 1, 1940, President Roosevelt presented a gold medal to Cohan. The medal had been authorized by Congress on June 29, 1936, for Cohan's authorship of "Over There" and "The Grand Old Flag."*

The line formed early for purchase of tickets to Oklahoma!, *the last legitimate stage presentation at the National before it was converted into a movie theatre. On Saturday, July 31, 1948, the National closed, victim of the theatre's racial policies which excluded blacks from the audience. At curtain call the cast sang "Auld Lang Syne."*

of widespread unemployment and jeopardizing the continuation of the eight-year-old stock company. However, the actors agreed to tax themselves to help pay for the extra musicians and continue the summer season, which would otherwise have ended after only two weeks. In order to aid the actors who had contributed to the musicians' salaries, the time-honored solution of a benefit was planned. On May 15, 1932, local critics and celebrities performed, and the evening was a financial success. The company survived and prospered.

By 1935 the *Washington Post* would claim that the National Theatre Players, as the summer stock company was called, had "become known as one of the foremost repertory companies in the United States."

Although the National was beset by union problems, threats of censorship, and enforcement of the District's stringent child labor laws, the theatre continued to draw outstanding productions. The lavishly staged *Victoria Regina*, starring Helen Hayes and Vincent Price, arrived in December, 1935. Mrs. Roosevelt led the applause on opening night, and the *Washington Daily News* reported that Miss Hayes's curtain calls were "limited only by her own fatigue." Miss Hayes had appeared at the National with William Gillette in the Charles Frohman production of Sir James Barrie's *Dear Brutus* 17 years earlier.

The 1930s also saw the appearances of Walter Hampden in *Cyrano de Bergerac, Hamlet, Richelieu,* and *Richard III*. The Theatre Guild brought such notable productions as *A Month in the Country, Green Grow the Lilacs* (later to return as *Oklahoma!*), *Mourning Becomes Electra*, and *Mary of Scotland*. The stage also glowed with the presence of Katharine Cornell, Florence Reed, Ralph Richardson, and Maurice Evans in *Romeo and Juliet*. John Gielgud starred with Judith Anderson and Lillian Gish in *Hamlet*.

The 1940s opened with Tallulah Bankhead in *The Little Foxes*, to be followed by Ethel Barrymore in one of her greatest roles as Miss Moffat in *The Corn is Green*. During the decade, the Theatre Guild returned with a number of productions, including *The Time of Your Life*, and Helen Hayes and Maurice Evans in *Twelfth Night*. Charles Coburn and Jesse Royce Landis starred in *The Merry Wives of Windsor*. The epoch-making production of *The Skin of Our Teeth* brought Tallulah Bankhead, Fredric March, Florence Eldridge, Montgomery Clift and E.G. Marshall to the National. In the cast of *The Three Sisters*, which included Judith Anderson, Ruth Gordon, Katharine Cornell, and Edmund Gwenn, was the novice actor Kirk Douglas. The musical theatre was well-represented at the National by grand operas, operettas, and popular Broadway musicals.

A special private performance of Lillian Hellman's *Watch On the Rhine* was given for President Roosevelt on January 25, 1942, because the child labor laws prevented the anti-Nazi drama from being performed for the public. So that *Life With Father* could play the National in February, 1944, the role of Harlan Day had to be written out of the script to obey these same laws.

THE CURTAIN FALLS

What fires, wars, financial panics, censorship, movies, and labor unions could not do—close the National—racial prejudice finally did. The segregation of black spectators into the upper areas of American theatres was an accepted practice long before the National Theatre opened in 1835. As early as January 19, 1768, a playbill for a New York performance announced that "Ladies and gentlemen will please send their servants to keep their places at four o'clock." When their masters arrived, the blacks were marshalled up to the gallery to await their "honours" at the close of the performance.

The situation in Washington was complicated by the presence of two classes of blacks—the slaves and the free blacks. The original Black Code of 1808 had been revised over the years, each revision placing more restrictions on the black population. In 1827 a stricter curfew prevented blacks from attending the theatre. Modifications to the code in 1835 that barred blacks from appearing on the streets without a permit after 10:00 p.m. inhibited theatre attendance. The code's severe restrictions on employment and personal liberties were attempts to limit the influx of free blacks into Washington.

Insensitivity toward blacks can be seen in the manner in which the *National Intelligencer* reported the burning of the National Theatre on March 5, 1845. Between 8:00 and 9:00, fire broke out in the oil room located near the rear of the building during a performance of *Beauty and the Beast*. Also scheduled that evening was a farce called *Stage Struck Nigger* and a performance of the Congo Melodists. The newspaper reported that the

cause of the fire was "a candle without a stick left burning on a table by a negro."

The Compromise of 1850 prohibited slave trade in Washington, and attacks on free blacks lessened in the local press. Once again the Black Code was modified, and although racial relations improved somewhat in Washington, segregation was maintained when the second National Theatre opened in 1850. Blacks were still relegated to the topmost gallery and the two boxes flanking the gallery were designated the "colored boxes."

The situation for blacks at the National still did not improve when the third National with its "colored parterre" opened in 1862. However, Ford's Theatre, the National's main competitor, excluded blacks entirely from its performances at this time. By 1873, when the fourth National opened, the accepted custom of excluding blacks entirely from the audience was followed.

The tense racial atmosphere in Washington is illustrated by the controversy surrounding the presentation of D.W. Griffith's masterpiece *The Birth of a Nation*, when it began a long run in 1916. Many claimed that the movie was "an incitement to riot" and urged the Commissioners to ban the film, just as they earlier banned the prize-fight film of Jack Johnson beating Jim Jeffries. When *Nation* returned to the National in the early twenties, the theatre's management played up the black-white conflict in advertising for the film. The film played to six weeks of capacity audiences.

Throughout the 1920s, the National Theatre's management remained determined to keep blacks out of the theatre. Because "passing" by light-skinned blacks was so common during the time, the National employed a black man to sit at the door and bounce those whose racial origins were undetectable to whites. According to the *Washington Tribune* of April 11, 1925, the black doorman was not despised by the light-skinned blacks because he was "only doing his job."

While *The Green Pastures* with its all-black cast was playing the National in February of 1933, The National Association for the Advancement of Colored People asked author Marc Connelly and producer Rowland Stebbans to withdraw the play before the completion of its run because the theatre was segregated and because actor Richard B. Harrison, who was playing De Lawd, was receiving threats. Stebbans responded that he would not interfere with the house policies of the National, and his Washington agent claimed that Harrison and the rest of the cast were eager to finish the run. As a compromise, blacks were admitted to a special benefit for the Elks on February 26 and again on March 2.

Anti-black sentiment in Washington affected the National Theatre in ways other than proscription of blacks from the auditorium. In February, 1934, the *Washington Tribune* reported that the National had decided to withdraw *They Shall Not Die,* which was based on the Scotsboro Case, because white theatregoers had protested so vigorously against it. Theatre manager Steve Cochran denied that racial prejudice had anything to do with the cancellation; he claimed that youngsters in the cast could not act in Washington because of the stringent child labor laws. However, information from New York confirmed that this major Broadway success, with its strong pro-black theme, had been forced to cancel its Washington run because of racial prejudice. *The School for Husbands* was substituted.

The no-black policy at the National was lifted for selected productions. When an announcement was made that blacks would be excluded from the production of George and Ira Gershwin's *Porgy and Bess* in March of 1936, pressure from a group of Howard University professors convinced manager Cochran to suspend the theatre's policy temporarily. Supporting the professors was the American Federation of Teachers Union. Further pressure was applied by the Theatre Guild and by Todd Duncan, former professor of music at Howard University, who was singing the role of Porgy. Blacks were also admitted on a limited basis for *As Thousands Cheer* in February, 1933, for one performance of *Pins and Needles* in December, 1938, for *This is the Army* in September, 1942, and for *Winged Victory* in March, 1945.

These productions, like other black social gains, were exceptions, and early in 1941 the nation's racial situa-

tion had not improved. A. Philip Randolph, head of the Brotherhood of Sleeping Car Porters, sent out a call for 50,000 blacks to march on Washington, hoping that President Roosevelt and Congress would become aware of job discrimination. By April the protest appeared a distinct possibility, and in June Mayor La Guardia of New York arranged a meeting between the black leaders, Mrs. Roosevelt, and government representatives.

Meetings at the White House during June produced an Executive Order on Fair Employment Practices signed by President Roosevelt. However, the Order did not apply to labor unions or private employers without defense contracts.

Racial restrictions continued at the National Theatre as in much of Washington. At this time Richard Wright's *Native Son,* directed by Orson Welles, was opening at the National. Entering a Washington restaurant with one of the white producers and a white woman, Wright was told that he could be served only in a car at the curb since the restaurant did not seat blacks.

Black resentment toward the National's racist policies was exacerbated when a sign appeared in the the-

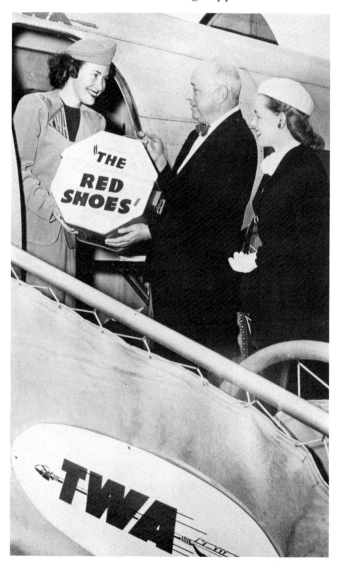

A print of the movie, "The Red Shoes," an acclaimed British art film, arrived in Washington via TWA on October 13, 1948. Two days later its American premiere drew a capacity crowd to the National, newly redecorated and renovated as a movie theatre.

atre's lobby stating that if tickets were presented by people prohibited from attending the theatre, admission would be denied and refunds refused. This was a way to counter a black strategy of arriving at the theatre with tickets purchased by whites, and when being refused admission, presenting the tickets for a refund when the curtain was about to go up and resale was impossible. When the theatre refused to make refunds, the Committee for Racial Democracy warned the National on December 6, 1946, that legal action would be taken.

Resentment and opposition to the segregationist policies continued to increase. Pickets protesting the theatre's policies started marching in front of the National on January 13, 1947, during a performance of *Blossom Time*. President Truman crossed the picket lines, but he later told reporters that he was not aware of the pickets at the time he attended the production.

Efforts to force management to change its segregationist policies increased on January 23, 1947, when it was announced that more than 20 theatre professionals, including Helen Hayes, Oscar Hammerstein II,

Frederic March, and Cornelia Otis Skinner had signed a boycott pledge against the National and the Lisner Auditorium of George Washington University. The pledge read:

I condemn and decry the practice of discrimination in the theatre as an action completely in disagreement with all basic principles of the profession.

As a first step to combat this evil, I will not knowingly contract to perform in any play in any theatre in the city of Washington which practices such discrimination toward either audience or performer.

Several days later, 36 playwrights signed a petition which stated that they would never allow their plays to be performed at the National until blacks were admitted. At the same time Edward Henderson filed a suit in the Municipal Court of the District of Columbia claiming that he was denied admission to the theatre solely because he was black. This was to be a test case

of the Civil Rights Act of 1875, which outlawed segregation in public areas. However, the suit was dismissed. The Supreme Court in 1883 had held that the 1875 law was unconstitutional because Congress could not create a code of municipal law for the regulation of private rights. Henderson appealed, but lost.

Concurrently five persons associated with the Committee for Racial Democracy filed suit against the National for ticket refunds. The theatre counter-charged that the tickets were bought fraudently as a "deliberate scheme to cause the theatre financial loss." During the trial, Edmund Plohn, manager of the National, claimed that blacks were excluded because their admission would be "distasteful" to the regular clientele and therefore financially harmful to the theatre. He stated that after a discussion with Police Superintendent Harvey B. Callahan about "the risks of mixed audiences," the theatre owners decided to maintain the segregationist policies. However, the plaintiffs won their suit and the National Theatre paid a judgment.

Pressure against the National continued to mount as Actors' Equity Association announced in April, 1947, that no member of the union could perform at the National unless the discrimination policies were abolished. The theatre was given until June, 1948, to comply with the order. On August 12, 1948, the National's management announced that it would not alter its segregationist stand unless integration policy throughout Washington was changed either by legal action or by mutual consent of business and civic groups.

The June deadline approached, the National's management remained adamant, and the theatre closed on July 31, 1948, with a farewell production of *Oklahoma!* that played to standing-room-only audiences. The theatre was converted into a movie house and the National reopened on October 16, 1948, with *The Red Shoes*. The National Theatre had closed once again, not because of fire, but because of racial prejudice.

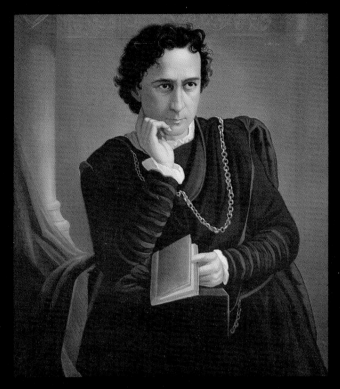

Edwin Booth made theatrical history with his production of **Hamlet,** *which ran for an unprecedented 100 nights in New York. Brother of the infamous John Wilkes Booth, Edwin retired from the stage for nine months after Lincoln's assassination. He brought* **Hamlet** *frequently to the National.*

Joseph Jefferson, III, seen here as Rip Van Winkle, made his stage debut in Washington at the age of four in a Jim Crow costume. Rip Van Winkle became his signature role, and he played it often at the National, where he was, at various times, doorman, stage manager, theatre manager, and star actor.

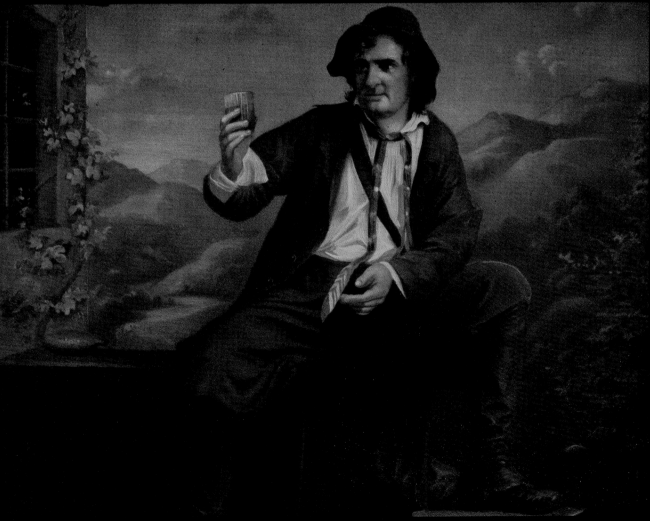

Major American musicals have been presented at the National, including Li'l Abner, *based on Al Capp's comic-strip characters, with Peter Palmer in the title role.*

Zero Mostel was the lead zany in A Funny Thing Happened on the Way to the Forum, *a show based on a ribald old Roman comedy.*

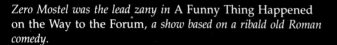

Robert Preston and Mary Martin charmed audiences with the more subdued appeal of a long-lasting marriage in I Do, I Do.

Torrid Latin dance flared in West Side Story, *one of the great creations of the American musical theatre. The show tried out in Washington at the National, where many details were set, including lighting effects ranging from cool street-blue to sizzling passion-red.*

Pearl Bailey, who grew up in Washington, stood proudly with her co-star Cab Calloway, and President and Mrs. Johnson, after a matinee performance of Hello, Dolly! Later that night Miss Bailey posed for LIFE magazine.

Carol Channing was the original Dolly in the musical, which tried out at the National. On one of her many return engagements, Channing made nightly curtain-call speeches which were of major importance in saving the National from the wrecking ball.

Determined to marry, Adelaide, played by Norma Donaldson in Guys and Dolls, *explains to her boyfriend, Nathan Detroit, played by Robert Guillaume, the psychic stress on the "female remaining single, just in the legal sense."*

Hair, *the quintessential rock musical of the iconoclastic Vietnam-War era, shot fusilades of high-decibel protests across the footlights to audiences of delighted youth and their nonplussed elders.*

CATS, *a musical based on T.S. Eliot's* Old Possum's Book of Practical Cats, *had surprisingly wide appeal in Washington. With a savvy combination of intriguing music and poetry, high-energy performances, inventive staging, and dazzling special effects, its seven-month run at the National was the longest in the theatre's history.*

ACT III:

Stellar Seasons

THE CURTAIN RISES

*D*uring the spring of 1949, while special-attraction films were still occasionally shown at the National, a distinguished group of Washingtonians convened to discuss the dearth of professional theatre in the nation's capital. *Washington Post* drama critic Richard L. Coe; Rev. Gilbert V. Hartke, O.P., founder of Catholic University's Speech and Drama Department; Congressmen Emanuel Celler and Jacob Javits of New York; Congressman John Blatnik of Minnesota; actress Frances Starr; impresario Patrick Hayes, and others, were determined to find an enlightened entrepreneur who could secure the National Theatre lease and admit black patrons.

When no such savior was forthcoming, the charismatic Fr. Hartke went to New York seeking the conversion of Marcus Heiman, the current lessee, but not even the dashing Dominican preacher could persuade Heiman to integrate. However, when Heiman's lease ran out in 1952, Broadway producers Richard Aldrich and Richard Myers secured control of the National and announced that in association with Robert Dowling they would open an integrated legitimate theatre.

Call Me Madam, chosen to reopen the theatre, boasted

A Chorus Line was played against periaktoi, triangular scenery devices first used in ancient Greek theatres. Covered with mirrors, they multiplied the effect of the chorus line in a top-hat-and-tails finale.

89

Helen Hayes, "First Lady of
the American Theatre," saw
her first play at the National.
She played the house many
times and returned in 1984 for
the theatre's reopening, making
a toast in the Helen Hayes
Gallery, where her official national portrait hangs.

not only Ethel Merman, reigning queen of musical comedy, but composer Irving Berlin, authors Howard Lindsay and Russel Crouse, choreographer Jerome Robbins, and director George Abbott. Merman's role, modeled after Washington party-giver Perle Mesta, gave the star a perfect vehicle to play in the nation's capital. Lee Shubert closed the show early in New York so that Merman could play a month in Washington before heading for Hollywood to re-create her role on film.

The opening night, May 5, 1952, was a triumph for art and social justice. The critics showered superlatives on Miss Merman, and the lure of the star, a capital-inspired musical, and the reopening of the long-dark National brought out a throng of prominent first-nighters including Senator Robert Taft, General George C. Marshall, and Alice Roosevelt Longworth.

Kentucky-born Edmund Plohn, who supervised the National in the twelve years preceding its spotty cinema era, returned as manager. Now at each performance he stood in the theatre lobby, impeccable in manner and attire, welcoming back the patrons. Two summers later he turned the management over to his young protege, Scott Kirkpatrick. Kirkpatrick became something of a legendary figure at the National, arriving as a second balcony usher, and leaving after 20 years' service as manager. Like his predecessor he greeted patrons at the theatre entrance nightly. Nattily turned out in a three-piece black suit with gold watch-chain in winter, and a seersucker suit or white palm beach with white shoes in summer, he epitomized Southern decorum.

Representing Theatre Guild subscriptions in Washington during the 1950s was the indefatigable Bess Davis Schreiner. A prodigious salesperson, she marketed so many tickets at reduced rates that the theatre began losing money and asked her to cut back. Schreiner studied the big seating charts in her office assiduously, committing to memory the seat locations of her clients. Wearing a picture hat, although they were scarcely in fashion, she was easy for panicked patrons to spot in the crowded lobby. There she unsnarled ticket mix-ups and soothed the upset. Subscribers who became too testy, however, were deftly reminded that the choicest locations were held tenaciously for *years* by Washington matrons who passed them on in their *wills* to their *dearest* friends, and anyone who coveted *those* seats would simply have to be patient . . . and long-lived. Schreiner was an energetic organizer and she established a Washington Play Series Committee to spread the gospel of theatregoing. Among her volunteers for 1952-1953 were mesdames Archbold, Biddle, Cafritz, de Morgenstierne, Frankfurter, Guggenheim, Kefauver, and Phillips.

Schreiner was devoted to the notion that young people should be encouraged to come to the theatre. In 1955 she established a half-price student subscription series in the second balcony: seats for nine plays were $8.85. The orchestra subscription for the same plays ran to $34.65. With her death a long family association with Washington theatre ended: Schreiner's father had ushered at Ford's Theatre on the evening Lincoln was killed. He and a young pal then sat across the street on the steps of the Petersen house where Lincoln lay dying. The two boys watched the grim ritual, disregarded by the procession of mourners who came and went on that wretched night.

THE WORKING THEATRE

The National had been made ready for motion pictures with a $75,000 rehabilitation. Air-conditioning was installed, and the "car-barn interior of cold dusty gray" had been repainted. The new pale-green-and-rose color scheme struck critic Richard Coe as "reformed Belle Watling decor." The theatre was again spruced up in 1956 when pale yellow damask was applied to the walls, and a house curtain similar in color hung to replace the "present drab curtain." The crowning and lasting feature of this redecoration was an enormous hand-carved wooden eagle placed above the proscenium arch. Painted white and set off by the yellow wall, the national emblem was flanked by ascending arcs of white stars, six on one side, seven on the other, celebrating the thirteen original colonies. The eagle replaced a pastoral mural which had topped the proscenium for many years. The mural's backing had decayed, and when workmen began to remove it, the artwork disintegrated.

Backdrops and large pieces of scenery—attached to pipe battens—are raised into the fly loft above a stage on sets of lines. The National is one of the few remaining "hemp houses," a theatre in which the lines are ropes tied to sand bags—rather than the steel cables controlled by iron weights or motors used in modern theatres. Traditionalists insist that the hemp-and-sand bag system gives stagehands more flexible and sensitive control than the newer methods of flying scenery.

Like all professional proscenium theatres, the National has an "asbestos curtain," a huge metal-framed panel designed to keep a stage fire from spreading to the auditorium. The curtain is hydraulically controlled. Its great water cylinder below the stage is among the last such devices still existing in any American theatre.

Actors applaud the "feel" of the auditorium, in which the farthest orchestra seat is only 55 feet from the stage. The National's mezzanine seating and steeply-tiered balcony present the performer with the immediacy of what Carol Channing called "an audience all pasted up there on the wall." The drum-shaped cantilevered boxes range down toward the proscenium on each side, gracefully linking playgoers and stage. Critic David Richards explains that the National is "Washington's only true road house, dating from days when Broadway shows took regularly to the provinces and the 91

Ethel Merman delighted Washington in Call Me Madam, *playing an ambassador modeled on Perle Mesta, the "Hostess with the Mostest."*

On the National Theatre program cover Peter Arno's cartoon celebrated "La Merm's" modish pompadour.

Carol Channing leapt to mega-carat stage stardom with "Diamonds Are a Girl's Best Friend" in Gentlemen Prefer Blondes. *She brought almost all of her stage shows to the National.*

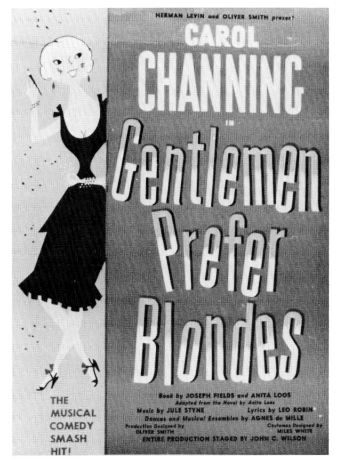

heartbreak and drama of tryouts were somehow more personal than they are in today's conglomerate world."

Performers frequently commended the acoustics of the auditorium in the years when actors were trained to be heard without amplification. If they were not heard, they were blamed: One critic complained that a British Juliet had "the voice of a mouse."

When a patron in 1958 criticized the National's acoustics, Manager Kirkpatrick was quick to defend a building

recognized for its marvelous acoustics throughout the architectural world. . . . Several of the departments of architecture of the large universities from time to time send their students to Washington on a field trip for the purpose of studying the structure of the National Theatre and to try to figure out the reasons for its marvelous acoustics.

Kirkpatrick speculated that the Tiber Creek, flowing through an aqueduct beneath the auditorium, forms a

Oliver Smith, who chose the vibrant color scheme for the National's 1984 redecoration, was co-producer and designer for Carol Channing's most celebrated success.

93

As Daisy Mae, Edith (later Edie) Adams was enthralled by strapping Peter Palmer, who played the title role in the musicalized version of Al Capp's comic strip, Li'l Abner.

Rosalind Russell led her stage nephew, and her live audience, to heady heights as the fantastic and free-thinking Auntie Mame.

resonating chamber beneficial to the theatre. He stressed that in recent remodelings care was taken "to keep every nook and cranny of the original McElfatrick design so as to take no chance on destroying any part of this acoustic gem." Ironically, Kirkpatrick added that "No artificial or mechanical means of increasing the volume of live voices at the National Theatre is ever used. Occasionally, the audience will see a sound box on each side of the proscenium arch, but these are used only for taped sound effects."

By the 1970s the "sound boxes" had evolved into multiple stereo speakers, and few actors in major roles performed unamplified. In 1984, 13 of the 22 performers in *CATS* were wired with microphones and hidden battery packs. The following year, at a performance of *42nd Street,* a tenor's amplified high note shattered the glasses of a patron.

The musicians' contract during the 1950s required that instrumentalists be engaged even for plays without music. An ensemble performed overture, intermission, and exit melodies (often old operetta favorites)

and fox trots. The effect was agreeable enough for sprightly comedies but disconcerting for drama when the travails of Willy Loman might be punctuated by "Tea For Two" at the *entr'acte.*

Some insight into post-World-War-II theatregoing, and a fascination with production details, is reflected in old stagebills. The listings for *Carnival* helpfully note: "Coca-Cola by the Coca-Cola Company, Donkey through Dawn Animal Agency, Inc., Dance notation by Myrna Shedlin and Allen Miles: accredited by Dance Notation Bureau. Candy by Lofts." The playbill in 1965 still advised patrons of the "racks for men's hats attached under seats," and admonished that "Tipping of this theatre's employees at any time is not permitted." It urged "for the safety of all that theatre patrons refrain from lighting matches in this theatre," and offered:

Alfred Lunt and Lynn Fontanne were elegant clairvoyants in
The Great Sebastians. *The couple first appeared together at the National and returned often as the reigning married royalty of the stage.*

In the 1950s and 1960s serious plays were not expected to sustain a run of more than one or two weeks, as they traveled from Baltimore to Washington and then to the south or west—or returned quickly to New York.

Playing opposite Miss Hasso, Eva LeGallienne was thunderously majestic as Queen Elizabeth I. Stately bearing and impeccable diction gave the role, and the production, bite and grandeur. LeGallienne played many shows at the National during her long career.

"Coats, umbrellas and parcels checked free of charge." The ticket envelope warned that "any person under the age of 17 must be accompanied by a parent or guardian."

WHITE HOUSE NEIGHBORS

Every president since 1835 has attended the National Theatre, with the exception of President Eisenhower, who did, however, attend when he was a General. Presidential families, too, have been frequent patrons. Eleanor Roosevelt was known to stroll over from the White House, handbag in hand, to pick up her own ticket at the box office. She frequently visited backstage after the performance, always solicitous for the actors. Franklin Roosevelt's visits were carefully planned to accommodate his wheelchair in the least conspicuous way. The President arrived by limousine in the alley behind the theatre, and from there his chair was rolled along an outside fire escape on the west side of the

building. On these occasions Jimmie Been—who worked at various jobs in the theatre for more than 40 years—was often stationed on the left side of the auditorium in the box which directly adjoins an exit. There he awaited a knock which would signal the Chief Executive's arrival on the fire escape outside. The house lights were then extinguished, the door opened, and the President was positioned by the glow of Been's flashlight. Often FDR was transferred to a chair brought from The White House, but on later visits his wheelchair was rolled into the box. When the President was settled, the curtain would rise and the stage lights came on.

After World War II most White House visits involved Secret Service arrangements made several days in advance. Nonetheless, the Trumans came over from the

Signe Hasso brought stormy elegance to her feisty portrayal of the doomed Mary, Queen of Scots, in a tour-de-force staging of Schiller's Mary Stuart.

Executive Mansion frequently, and with a minimum of fuss. Bess Truman was an inveterate matinee-goer. One week she attended six of the eight opera performances. At a sparsely attended matinee she led the applause, delighting a grateful cast. Mamie Eisenhower saw almost all the plays at the National during her White House years, and later motored down from Gettysburg for matinees.

John F. Kennedy had been a National Theatre subscriber both as congressman and as senator. With his election to President, the Secret Service preferred that he sit in a box which separated him from the audience, rather than use the orchestra seats which the Kennedys had heretofore enjoyed. The two front boxes at the left side of the auditorium were combined and enlarged with a two-and-a-half-foot extension to create the "Star Box." On occasion when the President came to the theatre his favorite rocking chair was sent ahead and placed here. Although the Kennedys relinquished the four center seats in Row G to which they had subscribed, they sometimes requested those seats again, and sat there on their last visit to the theatre.

The impulsive Lyndon Johnson arrived on short notice one afternoon to see Pearl Bailey in *Hello, Dolly!* Bailey, who had grown up in Washington and frequently appeared on the bill at the Howard Theatre and the Sylvan Theatre on Rhode Island Avenue, was delighted to be opening her all-black company of the hit show in her home town. "It will be a treat," she said. "You don't think when you're a little girl of three that you'll be opening some day in a Broadway show where you used to live!"

The Johnsons arrived just before the second act at a sold-out matinee. There was no democratic way to unseat paying customers, even for The First Couple. Chairs were set up in the right aisle, and the President of the United States and his wife sat in the aisle adjacent to rows E and F.

Mrs. Johnson led the standing ovation that followed the performance, and Bailey waved a welcome to her distinguished guests. Adding to the unorthodoxy of the visit, The Chief Executive headed backstage. Bailey took Mrs. Johnson's hand and led her and the President out onto the light-bulb-studded runway in front of the orchestra pit. The thrilled audience joined the star in singing "Hello, Lyndon!" to the tune of the show's theme song. Bailey then quieted the house and saluted Lady Bird: "Dolly arranges everything: No man can stop in without his wife! This show is full of love!" The President added: "I just wish it were possible for everyone everywhere at the end of a long hard week they've gone through to have the treat we had here this afternoon!" The curtain rose and fell three times on this unique trio: a President, a First Lady, and a musical-comedy star who rose from cabaret singer to become a member of the United States delegation to the United Nations—and a world-wide "Roving Am-

bassador of Love." Bailey's big day was not over, however. At a photo call after the performance that night, *LIFE* magazine shot pictures of the show. Carol Channing had previously appeared as Dolly on the magazine's cover. Now Bailey had that honor, setting for *Hello, Dolly!* a record as the only show twice pictured on the cover of *LIFE*.

President and Mrs. Nixon, who often attended plays in New York on weekends, made their first presidential visit to the National to see movie star Debbie Reynolds in a revival of the Broadway musical, *Irene*. A curbside crowd was waiting at curtain time when a black limousine with fluttering presidential flags swept up and the Chief Executive bounded out to shake hands and greet the delighted bystanders. Secret Service agents escorted the presidential party to their aisle seats in the orchestra.

President and Mrs. Carter saw Liv Ullmann as *Anna Christie,* and paid their respects backstage after the performance. Later Ullmann returned from a trip to Africa and spoke eloquently about world hunger to an audience of children one Saturday morning at the National.

PLAYERS

The marquee of the National Theatre has borne the names of many of the great actors of the English-speaking theatre.

Among them are Henry Fonda who appeared first in 1934 and finally 40 years later; and Rex Harrison, who first played opposite his wife, the charming Lilli Palmer, and returned 27 years later in 1980 opposite the ever-glamorous Claudette Colbert.

Other National Theatre alumni after mid-20th century include Brian Bedford, Charles Boyer, Tom Courtenay, Maurice Evans, Cedric Hardwicke, Laurence Harvey, Van Heflin, Louis Jourdan, Roddy McDowall, Raymond Massey, Barry Nelson, Laurence Olivier, Anthony Perkins, Christopher Plummer, Tyrone Power, Claude Rains, Cyril Ritchard, and George C. Scott. Richard Burton starred with Helen Hayes and Susan Strasberg in *Time Remembered,* and Ralph Richardson and John Gielgud glistened in *The School for Scandal.* Comedians John Belushi, Art Carney, Chevy Chase, James Coco, Buster Keaton, Bert Lahr, Sam Levene, Dudley Moore, Carroll "Archie Bunker" O'Connor, and Phil Silvers appeared, and Woody Allen played opposite Diane Keaton.

Singers, too, brought their signature musicals to the National. Among them were Alfred Drake in *Kismet,* Jerry Orbach in *Carnival,* and Richard Kiley in *Man of La Mancha,* a show he opened in New York, but which played six engagements at the National before Washington saw him in the role.

Some of the "first appearances" were in quite minor

roles: Jason Robards did not have featured billing in *Stalag 17* in 1953, and Walter Matthau had only a small part in the serious anti-war thriller, *The Burning Glass*, in 1954. Elliott Gould, later to marry Barbra Streisand and star in films, sang in the chorus of *Irma La Douce* in 1960. Playing supporting roles with Katharine Cornell in 1953 were Lorne Greene and Robert Culp.

Warren Beatty made his major stage debut in William Inge's *A Loss of Roses*, which played the National in 1959 before going to New York, where it survived only two weeks. He did not seem promising to Richard Coe, who noted that "the evidently inexperienced young actor fails to make the character completely dramatic." Beatty was not new to the National. The son of Arlington Realtor Ira Beaty, he had worked at the theatre in 1955, the same year that he was named to the "All-Suburban Washington High School Football Team." His sister, Shirley MacLaine, who preceded him into films,

A young Robert Redford, not yet a motion picture megastar, gets a cool reaction from his co-star in a scene from the comedy, Sunday in New York.

changed her family name completely. Warren settled for the change of Beaty to Beatty.

Grease came to the National with Jeff Conaway, later seen on TV in "Taxi," as Danny Zuko. Playing the smaller role of Doody was a chunky, brown-haired John Travolta, who would later disco to fame in the film, *Saturday Night Fever*. Teetotaler Travolta dragooned his cohorts up to a Natural Foods store on F Street between shows to quaff carrot juice and munch crunchy salads.

The great leading ladies who took their shows on the road from the 1950s through the 1970s appeared at the National, some a number of times. The glittering roster includes Judith Anderson, Tallulah Bankhead, Gertrude Berg, Shirley Booth, Carol Channing, Katharine Cornell, Ruth Gordon, Tammy Grimes, Julie Harris, Helen Hayes, Katharine Hepburn, Eva LeGallienne, Beatrice Lillie, Mary Martin, Geraldine Page, Margaret Sullavan, and Margaret Webster. Bankhead's father, Speaker of the House of Representatives, would "buy out the entire orchestra and invite the whole Congress to come see his daughter," recalls Adolphe Meyer,

The theatre interior, remodeled in 1922, showed faux-stone walls and an ornate curtain in a sketch featured in a Washington Post *article published upon the theatre's reopening. The paneled mural above the proscenium and much of the ornate plasterwork no longer exist. The drum-shaped boxes, although modified, remain in place today.*

who began checking wraps at the National in 1924, and was still working in the theatre box office 61 years later.

Helen Hayes, born in Washington, serves as honorary chairman of The National Theatre Corporation. She saw her first play in this house, where she has appeared many times. In 1955 she starred with Mary Martin and George Abbott in Thornton Wilder's *The Skin of Our Teeth.* The director was Alan Schneider, who had begun his career in Washington as a teacher at Catholic University and a director at Arena Stage. Hayes's role as the eternally optimistic mother in this production was, in critic Tom Donnelly's words, "one of her best performances, which is the equivalent of a ton of superlatives." Richard Coe agreed that it was

"as brilliant a performance as she has ever given." In 1971 Helen Hayes retired from the stage after a farewell performance in Washington at Catholic University in Eugene O'Neill's *Long Day's Journey Into Night.*

Among others who played the National were Gwen Verdon, and Barbara Bel Geddes of TV's "Dallas." Eileen Brennan, while working in Washington, had appeared in productions at Georgetown University and Olney Theatre. She starred at the National in *The Miracle Worker* and returned to create the role of Irene Molloy in *Hello, Dolly!* Later, Elizabeth Ashley appeared, as did the virtuoso-voiced Geraldine Page, who played opposite her husband, Rip Torn, in *Sweet Bird of Youth.* National Theatre alumnae from Hollywood include Lauren Bacall, Anne Baxter, Arlene Francis, Audrey Hepburn, Celeste Holm, Jennifer Jones, Deborah Kerr, Viveca Lindfors, Lorna Luft, Gloria Swanson, and, making her American stage debut, Angela Lansbury in *Hotel Paradiso.*

In 1960 Julie Harris starred in *Little Moon of Alban,* the story of a nurse whose fiance's death allows her to

Scott Kirkpatrick, manager of the National for 20 years before his retirement in 1974, admires a plaque honoring the Bess Davis Schreiner for her years of service in subscription ticket sales.

The parade which racketed down the long stairways to the street was led by a high school principal from Sayreville, New Jersey, who ordered the walkout because she was shocked by the play's innuendos. "It was my duty!" she explained tearfully, as she marshalled the teenagers onto their buses and headed away into the night.

Applause!—the musical about an actress who wins Broadway's coveted Tony award—came to the theatre with Eleanor Parker. Having severely sprained an ankle prior to her Washington appearance, she began the seven-week run in great discomfort, with painkillers at-the-ready backstage. Ticket sales were off and the road-weary actors were depressed until they saw Parker forging gamely ahead through dance routines which aggravated a foot in need of rest. At the last Saturday matinee her pain escalated, and the star dropped in a faint as the curtain fell on Act One. She revived and struggled through the second act and that night's final performance. At the curtain call one of the "gypsies," the chorus singers and dancers whose work is especially celebrated in *Applause!*, presented to a tearful Parker the Tony-Award trophy used as a prop in the show. The cast had affixed to it an engraved plaque dedicating it to the heroic star who had inspired them all with her courage.

As leading ladies came and went, the theatre staff noted contrasts in the grandeur and simplicity of Hollywood queens and Broadway babies, TV personalities and new-famed ingenues. Exquisite Vivien Leigh entertained the actors at a sumptuous after-show supper-dance on the candle-lit terrazzo mezzanine. Sada Thompson, on the other hand, is remembered for her back-to-basics simplicity. She arrived one morning at the theatre and offered to help type and answer telephones. "You never know, in this business, what's coming along," she mused. "I like to keep up my secretarial skills." She spent the day in the theatre offices, occasionally taking telephone calls from unsuspecting patrons who would be applauding her on stage that evening.

Two great married couples of the American theatre—Alfred Lunt and Lynn Fontanne, Hume Cronyn and Jessica Tandy—were seen often at the National. The Lunts' first stage appearance anywhere together took place in 1919 in a summer season at the National with the George C. Tyler Stock Company. The play was *Made of Money* by Richard Washburn Child, later United States ambassador to Italy during the Mussolini regime. The cast of 27 included a dozen showgirls who modeled haute couture in a salon to which a dashing Lunt took the glamorous Fontanne to shop. Humid weather deterred playgoers from attending these historic perform-

By the mid-20th Century, the front of the National Theatre Building had been stripped of almost all architectural ornament, leaving an unadorned theatre entrance in a Bauhaus-bland facade.

fall in love with a dashing young lieutenant. Playing the thankless role of the doomed fiance was young Robert Redford, noted by Richard Coe as among "several who stand out." Redford returned the following year, now sharing top billing with Pat Stanley in the pre-Broadway try-out of *Sunday in New York*, a light comedy featuring some mildy risqué repartee. Toward the end of the first act, Redford and his co-star had a romantic scene followed by a blackout. When the lights came back up the couple wore bathrobes, but their dialogue revealed that "nothing really happened when the lights were off." Suddenly, as if by signal, 147 patrons in the uncarpeted upper balcony rose and headed for the exits. Redford and Stanley, startled by the clatter of trampling feet, thought the balcony might be collapsing. The performance stopped as the frightened audience, necks craned, peered up into the darkness.

Julie Harris' rich but husky voice gave naive and affecting vulnerability to her portrayal of St. Joan of Arc, as poetically depicted in The Lark, *adapted from the French of Jean Anouilh.*

ances, and poor ticket sales resulted in cancellation of the remainder of the planned season. The company then withdrew to New York. The Lunts, however, returned many times to the National, insuring their impeccable performances by climbing to the balcony at rehearsal to check vocal projection, acoustics, and lighting.

Hume Cronyn made his first professional appearance at the National playing a one-line walk-on for $25 a week. He returned in many plays with Jessica Tandy

but in *Hadrian VII* he performed without her. Some nights he sat on the lobby stairs chatting with the ushers before showtime. Tandy visited, bringing boxes of cream chocolates to the staff. She came without Cronyn in *Five Finger Exercise*, Peter Shaffer's first play, in its American premiere at the National under John Gielgud's direction. Tandy had played Ophelia to Gielgud's Hamlet in London exactly 25 years earlier. Later, Tandy Cronyn, daughter of Jessica and Hume, sang at the National in *Company*.

Vivien Leigh and Mary Ure, one garbed in claret, one in white, played warring spirits in the brightly cerebral Duel of Angels, *by Jean Giraudoux, also a translation from the French.*

STAR ATTRACTIONS

Producers often brought to Washington plays dealing with presidents, Congress, and the manners and *mores* of the republic. Franklin Roosevelt saw himself parodied at the National in the musical *I'd Rather Be Right,* and was portrayed later in *Sunrise at Campobello* and again in *Annie.* The Senate's opposition to a presidential candidate for Secretary of State is the subject of *Advise and Consent,* which arrived in 1960. "No play in recent memory," noted Richard Coe, "has come to Washington with such vast local interest. The run is sold out."

The post-Civil-war events portrayed in *The Andersonville Trial* actually took place in the Court of Claims, just a few blocks from the National where they were reenacted 95 years later. Gore Vidal in 1960 wrote *The Best Man,* which deals with the selection of a presidential candidate at a political convention. Vidal wrote another political play, *Weekend,* which came to the National in 1968, prior to Broadway. The play is set in the Washington home of a Senator, who was played by John Forsythe. It was not successful, but one performance brought to the theatre Senators Jacob Javits and Howard Baker, Representative—later Vice-President—George Bush, and from New York, Paul Newman and Joanne Woodward, all of whom gathered for a late supper after the show.

Mr. President, Irving Berlin's tribute to the highest office in the land, arrived while John F. Kennedy was in the White House. Word that he and Jacqueline would attend the $100-a-seat Opening Night Gala sent Potomac excitement to fever pitch. Mail orders poured in with a cascade of blank checks even before ticket prices for the remaining performances were announced. For the black-tie opening, designers festooned the theatre

Barricades were set up to make a path among well-wishers who waited in the cold to cheer the bright young First Couple of the "New Frontier" as they departed for an after-performance supper at the British Embassy.

Gold pasteboard tickets admitted the distinguished and excited black-tie gathering which shared the preview of Irving Berlin's White House musical with President and Mrs. John F. Kennedy. Longtime patrons of the National, the Kennedys invited many stars to perform at The White House.

Carol Lawrence, a neophyte when West Side Story *was in pre-Broadway tryout at the National, returned as a star to serenade Empress Farah of Iran and Perle Mesta, guests at "The Elms," the residence of Vice President and Mrs. Lyndon Johnson, and formerly Mme. Mesta's home.*

with patriotic bunting, and hung lithographs and photographs of the 34 former Chief Executives. President Kennedy missed the first act but joined the First Lady for the second. Nanette Fabray, playing the First Lady onstage, was aware of commotion in the Star Box as aides scurried about in the tense atmosphere preceding the Cuban Missile Crisis.

In the audience for the musical hit, *1776*, with its singing-and-dancing Continental Congress, were many *bona-fides* from The Hill, wistfully enjoying the lyrical portrait of their forebears.

In 1976 came the pre-Broadway tryout of *1600 Pennsylvania Avenue*, an ambitious Bicentennial salute. With a score by Leonard Bernstein, book and lyrics by Alan Jay Lerner, and $900,000 in backing from Coca-Cola, (the first commercial giant to act as sole investor in a Broadway show), hopes were high. A juxtaposition of the lives of First Families throughout history with those of their black servants gave the work a certain liberal cachet; but the show lagged where it should have leaped, and the notices were unfavorable. Directors were changed and eventually the play was "co-directed, staged and choreographed" by Gilbert Moses and George Faison. Faison, recently involved in the Broadway success of *The Wiz*, was a young choreographer who had matured while appearing in productions of Washington's American Light Opera Company. He added a dazzling dance opening to *1600*, but the show expired in a deadly shuffle of good intentions which no amount of fast-stepping could quicken.

Great classics of the English-speaking stage were seen with some regularity at the National, sometimes in a repertory of several plays, the whole engagement lasting from one to three weeks, often sold out in advance.

In 1957 The Old Vic presented four Shakespeare plays in a two-week repertory. Actors Paul Rogers and John Neville received keys to the city. Rogers noted that Lilian Bayliss, founder of The Old Vic,

always dreamed of a time when the Waterloo Road players would perform in the capital of the United States. Monday night at the National found a very curious atmosphere backstage. Someone remarked that though *Richard II* has had several hundred performances, tonight suddenly has the feeling of an opening night. We all agreed he was right.

In 1964, celebrating Shakespeare's 400th Anniversary, Paul Scofield triumphed as King Lear. The *Washington Post* called the opening night "a memorable one

The symbolic figure of a ghostly musician recurs throughout the musical Fiddler on the Roof, *and was used in its advertising. This enormously popular show brought Zero Mostel to Washington for a tryout. The Broadway-bound company had anxious moments when Mostel collapsed onstage midway through one performance, but star and cast revived and the production rose to resounding glory.*

107

1776: THE DRAMA OF GOVERNMENT

Politics and patriotism have always played well in Washington. Capital audiences are especially alert to the nuances of plays dealing with the federal establishment. *1776* won the Tony Award, Broadway's highest honor, as Best Musical in 1969, beating out *Hair* at a time when patriotic fervor had been much dampened by the Vietnam War. Many in the audience, including members of Congress, were keenly sympathetic to the legislative frustrations endured by their stage counterparts as the latter wrangled over details of the Declaration of Independence.

Rex Everhart was Benjamin Franklin in the musical, his makeup ingeniously created to evoke the great statesman.

American democracy was portrayed as an emerging eaglet on the show's handbill.

As 1776 celebrated the American Revolution, the National's hired ushers rebelled against management's plan to replace them with volunteers. The plan was quickly dropped.

Facsimile documents, accurate down to the finest detail, were signed onstage just five blocks from The National Archive, where the originals are on display.

A MUSICAL FOR THE AGE OF AQUARIUS

Just as earlier audiences had been shocked by Ibsen's epoch-making plays, so were many theatregoers of the Vietnam era startled by the outrageous lyrics and counterculture shenanigans of the musical *Hair*. Evolved from the mores and manners of the hippie culture, the show was iconoclastic in outlook and audacious in concept. Thematically, it seemed a blend of charming innocence and near-treasonable anarchy. Dramatically, it jettisoned the clear plot-line which had been the stalwart hallmark of American musical theatre.

Eager ticket-buyers queued up long before the box office opened.

A Hair-y official in a rya-rug coat, and a protester in a business suit, epitomized the clashing forces at the heart of the play.

Vigorous staging and youthful exuberance made Hair *a kaleidoscope of high-voltage montages.*

A lucky trio celebrated their purchase of the first available tickets.

Hair *ushered in "The Age of Aquarius" with its bold lyrics and
the first frontal nudity ever seen on the stage of the august
National Theatre. The show's book and lyrics were by two iconoclastic young men who knew Washington: one as a university
student, one as a soldier.*

Time-defying Claudette Colbert and urbane Rex Harrison teamed up for a return to the National in The Kingfisher. *Audiences were enchanted with the impeccably-groomed display of civility from two long-time stage and film favorites.*

in Washington theatre history," which concluded with "a ten-minute standing ovation."

Foreign troupes brought to Washington the theatre and dance of other nations. Ireland's "Dublin Players" visited, and an English-Yiddish musical revue as well. The exotic expatriate and internationally celebrated chanteuse, St. Louis-born Josephine Baker, also came "direct from Paris" to sing in many languages, with young Geoffrey Holder dancing in her company.

Chekhov plays presented a picture of Russia; and Germany was represented when Eva LeGallienne played a *sturm-und-drang* Elizabeth I in an English adaptation of Schiller's *Maria Stuart* with Signe Hasso in the title role. Le Gallienne returned in the production playing against TV celebrity Faye Emerson, uncharacteristically cast as the doomed Queen Mary.

Operas continued to be popular at the National. *Porgy and Bess* played four weeks in 1952 prior to a tour abroad. In the cast were children, banned from Washington stages since 1928, but now by a revision of law permitted to appear. The youngsters were an eight year-old boy and girl. Richard Coe, who had long campaigned for the child actors, and President Truman, who had just signed Representative Emanuel Celler's bill allowing them to act, led the cheers on opening night. Appearing "in her first major role" was Leon-

tyne Price as "a Bess of vocal glory and physical earthiness, a complete realization of the heroine." William Warfield, who married Price later on this tour, played Porgy, and Cab Calloway left his band to sing for the first time Sportin' Life, the role Gershwin created with him in mind. Also in the cast was Washington soprano Helen Thigpen, whose rendition of "My Man's Gone Now" was much admired. The production went on to Berlin, Vienna, Paris and London, and after 16 months in Europe returned the following year to the National, with Price, Calloway, Thigpen and the two children—now nine years old—still in their roles!

The Metropolitan Opera National Company brought grand opera to Washington, and The *D'Oyly Carte* Gilbert and Sullivan troupe played the National several times.

The American Ballet Theatre came in 1952 and again in 1954, when Alicia Alonso headed a company performing Jerome Robbins' *Fancy Free*, Agnes de Mille's *Fall River Legend*, and *Swan Lake*. The latter had been seen the previous year when Mia Slavenska and Frederic Franklin brought their 24-member company to Washington and also played one-act versions of *The Nutcracker* and *A Streetcar Named Desire*. The Royal Winnipeg Ballet of Canada with guest artist Alicia Markova also visited, as did the sadly short-lived *Harkness Ballet*.

Antonio Ruiz's *Ballets de Madrid* brought clicking heels and castanets to the stage in 1965, and his successor returned seven years later with his own *Antonio Gades Spanish Dance Company*. More Latin dance was featured by the *Ballet Internacional de Caracas. Les Ballets Africans,*

In Irene, *vivacious Debbie Reynolds danced atop a passel of pianos, and crouched beneath one as well.*

HITS AND MISSES

national ensemble of the Republic of Guinea, played four engagements between 1959 and 1968. The program included feverish tribal rituals, dramatic story-line dances, stilt-walkers, fire-eaters, and prodigious athletic feats.

America's flamboyant all-male "travesti ballet," *Trockadero de Monte Carlo,* played to rollicking houses. The company, whose spoofs were dependent upon their quite solid dance technique, included Ida Neversayneva, Igor Teupleze, Ludmila Beaulemova, and Suzina LaFuzziovitch, sporting a "5 o'clock shadow." The ingenious molecular acrobatics of *Pilobolus Dance Theater* were seen in the 1970s, and *Dancin',* Bob Fosse's frenetic dance extravaganza, came to the National in 1980.

HITS AND MISSES

As a major tryout town, Washington saw the birth pangs of major successes of the American theatre, and the death throes of failures. There was little doubt that *Auntie Mame* with Rosalind Russell was a hit show: Fifteen performances were sold out in advance, and the play received unanimous raves from the critics. Likewise *Li'l Abner* was an evident winner at its Washington world premiere, as was *Irma la Douce.*

Judy Holliday, who had charmed Washington in *Bells Are Ringing* at the peak of her career in 1959, returned four years later in *Hot Spot.* A comedy inspired by the Peace Corps, the tryout was doomed to fail in spite of the star's valiant perseverance. The usually vivacious Holliday seemed already enervated by the illness which would soon claim her life.

At the National, *A Funny Thing Happened on the Way to the Forum,* with Zero Mostel, was changed from sow's ear to silk purse by the sagacious addition of one musical number called "Comedy Tonight." This bouncy new opening set an upbeat tone which launched the bawdy farce on its zany trajectory. Mostel returned to Washington to try out *Fiddler On The Roof.* At the third performance Mostel sang "If I Were a Rich Man," and collapsed.

The curtain fell and standby Paul Lipson, sans understudy rehearsal, completed the performance. Mostel recovered and the show went on to become a Broadway hit. It returned to Washington four years later with Lipson, his name now above the title, playing the lead.

A Patriot For Me came from London in 1969 for its American premiere. The John Osborne drama of the Austro-Hungarian Empire featured blackmail, revenge, a fatal duel, a drag ball, and the hallowed National's first male nudity, rear view. The star was Maximilian Schell, who had made his American debut ten years earlier at the National opposite Celeste Holm in *Interlock.*

In this theatre the light cues were set and Jerome Robbins' choreography polished for the Bernstein/Sondheim *West Side Story.* Other successful tryouts were *I Do! I Do!* with Mary Martin and Robert Preston, *Cactus*

Flower starring Lauren Bacall and Barry Nelson, Neil Simon's *The Sunshine Boys*, and the musical *Promises, Promises*, directed by Robert Moore, a Washingtonian whose career blazed on Broadway before his untimely death.

When the revival of *Irene* opened in 1973 all was not yet smooth, and Debbie Reynolds made a curtain speech to beg the audience's indulgence. The show pulled together when an elaborate number was conceived in which pianos rolled about the stage, Reynolds strutting atop them with a chorus of prancing men. Upon arrival of the prop pianos in Washington, the number was choreographed at an all-night session. Everyone present sensed it was "right," and the show had its hit number. In the chorus of this show was Reynold's daughter, Carrie Fisher, who later rocketed to cinematic fame in *Star Wars*.

Carol Channing's incomparable talent could not save *The Vamp* or *Lorelei* enroute to Broadway, but she triumphed in *Hello, Dolly!*, which came to the National from Detroit. However, this show also arrived in trouble. Richard Coe's review helped convince David Merrick to jettison the costly costumes and props from a weak first-act ending and substitute an equally expensive replacement. Seamstresses stitched overtime, new orchestrations were penned, and in the crowded second-floor mezzanine of the theatre, new blocking began. At the final performance in Washington the jubilant "Before the Parade Passes By" was introduced and suddenly everything gelled. "The change cost Merrick $40,000," remembers Coe, "but it made him millions."

Show Boat, which had its world premiere at the National in 1927, steamed in again in 1980, co-produced by The New National Theatre Corporation and Wolf Trap Farm Park for the Performing Arts.

More colorful in some cases than the memorable triumphs are recollections of those vanished shows which arrived amid great expectations only to suffer ignominious oblivion on Broadway or indeed collapse before ever reaching the fabled rialto. Shirley Booth brought two unsuccessful try-outs, *Miss Isobel* and the musical *Juno*. *Nature's Way*, a comedy by Georgetown novelist Herman Wouk, was spurned by Washington audiences which included his friends and neighbors. Novelist Leon Uris saw the musical *Ari*, based on his book *Exodus*, similarly scorned, and columnist Art Buchwald's *Sheep on the Runway* scarcely fared better. *Handful of Fire* is remembered almost soley because Arthur Miller's sister, Joan Copeland, appeared. *Fun City*, starring its co-author, Joan Rivers, barged on to New York after its National visit, and promptly capsized.

In 1976 Jerry Lewis came through Washington in quest of his "life-long dream" to conquer Broadway. The vehicle chosen for his debut was a revival of *Hellzapoppin'*, a zany musical revue updated to suit his style. The show folded in Boston and Lewis called it "the lowest point of my show-business career." Two years later Gene Barry, TV's Bat Masterson, after an absence of 26 years, returned to the musical stage in *Spotlight*, which was extinguished at the end of its Washington run.

No Washington try-out is more deliciously nor maliciously recalled than the incomparably disastrous *Mata Hari*, David Merrick's failed adventure in espionage and opulence. Merrick was both a brilliant producer and the tyrant *terrible* of the theatre, and his latest extravaganza was breathlessly awaited. It was billed as "the most expensive musical ever risked." Jo Mielziner designed 30 period settings and Irene Sharaff created 300 dazzling costumes. Marisa Mell, an Austrian actress elevated from American anonymity to title billing, was to wear a $150,000 wardrobe of seductive gowns. Pernell Roberts, a one-time University of Maryland and Arena Stage actor who had gone on to fame as Adam on TV's "Bonanza," returned to Washington as Mell's leading man.

Glitterati crowded the theatre for a benefit preview—but fiasco waited in the wings. The curtain was late,

Mata Hari had a plot full of intrigue, an exotic star, lovely costumes, and elaborate sets, but not what it takes to make a successful musical. The show was a major failure in its highly publicized tryout at the National.

Smiles, spangles, and the star's charisma were all for naught as Jerry Lewis' version of Hellzapoppin' *tried out in Washington and was found lacking the magic which spells critical success.*

and Merrick stepped before the footlights to assuage audience angst. The show finally got underway at 9:00 and lasted more than three hours. Hollywood's Vincente Minnelli was returning to stage direction for the first time in 25 years, having directed cinema musicals such as the impressive Oscar-winners *An American in Paris* and *Gigi*. He had staged *Mata Hari* with the eye for shimmering detail which distinguished his lovely films. Two days before the preview he sat stationing soldiers meticulously on the stage like mosaic tiles until a ravishing warscape was framed. At the dress rehearsal he re-ran one scene because Miss Mell carried her beaded bag wrong side front. But the dynamics of the Broadway metier now eluded him, and in performance the impeccable stage-pictures paraded leadenly as the pace lagged and the glistening juggernaut ground down to a crawl. A Swiss chalet set on two platforms separated inexplicably, leaving the hero stranded mid-stage and mid-scene, as Mata Hari rolled haplessly into the wings. Next a recently re-choreographed sequence went awry as disoriented dancers collided in confusion. Then an unanticipated light cue suddenly revealed Miss Mell onstage en deshabille. Finally came the denouement. Funsters who happened to be present relished the moment wickedly for years thereafter. Condemned for treason, Mata Hari faced a firing squad. The salvo struck, she slumped, and the attending physician solemnly pronounced her dead. But, Alas! She raised a hand to her surely fevered brow and began to rise before the blackout. The planned poignancy of the moment, and all hope for *Mata Hari,* vanished in a volley of laughter, and the show closed in Washington. Merrick sent the costly paraphernalia of the ill-fated spectacle to storage—all except three of his star's exquisite beaded gowns: They had been stolen the night before her final performance.

Most plays of the 1950s were blind to the plight of minorities, but the enlarging black middle class began to discover black plays at the National in the 1960's. *A Raisin in the Sun*, by Lorraine Hansberry, is a landmark piece. The tormented but stoic family in the explosively well-made drama gripped the attention and sympathy of both whites and blacks when it first played the National, and again when the musical version *Raisin—*

BLACKS TAKE CENTER STAGE

American blacks emerged from the political turmoil of the 1960s and '70s with improved social status. A number of new plays about blacks, and old shows revived with all-black casts, found wide popularity in Washington, a city with a population which is mostly black. Afro-American lifestyles were portrayed with fervor and fancy by talented performers, who trod the boards with a refreshing confidence for integrated audiences who saw themselves, or their fellow Americans, in a new light.

The bedraggled plant propped up and nurtured by the heroine of Lorraine Hansberry's A Raisin in the Sun *was a symbol of the undaunted courage and hope of a valiant ghetto matriarch.*

James Earl Jones, appearing as Paul Robeson in a one-man show, kept on his dressing-room table a photo of Robeson as Eugene O'Neill's Emperor Jones. *Alongside the make-up are diet supplements, which many health-conscious actors use diligently to maintain the stamina necessary for stage performances.*

DON GREGORY presents

JAMES EARL JONES

as

PAUL ROBESON

The New Play by

PHILLIP HAYES DEAN

Scenery and Lighting by
H.R. POINDEXTER

Costume Design by
NOEL TAYLOR

Directed by

CHARLES NELSON REILLY

AN INTERNATIONAL CINEGRAPH: CREATIVE IMAGE PRODUCTION

4 Weeks Only! Mon. Dec. 5 thru Sat. Dec. 31

NATIONAL THEATRE

1321 E St., N.W., Washington, D. C. 20004
Box office opens Nov. 21 · Phone: 628-3393
Mon. thru Sat. Eves. at 8:00; Wed. & Sat. Mats. at 2:00
Opening Night curtain at 7:00

Prices: Mon. thru Thurs. Eves. and Sat. Mats. Orch. $10.90, Balc.
$10.50, 10.00, 9.50; 2nd Balc. $8.00, 7.50, 6.00. Fri. and Sat.
Eves. Orch. $12.50; Balc. $12.00, 11.50, 11.00; 2nd Balc. $9.50,
8.50, 7.00. Wed. Mats. Orch. $9.50; Balc. $9.00, 8.50, 8.00; 2nd
Balc. $6.50, 5.50, 5.00. Sat. New Year's Eve Dec. 31 Orch. $14.50;
Balc. $14.00, 13.50, 13.00; 2nd Balc. $11.00, 10.00, 9.00

Group Sales: (202) 634-7201

Instant Charge: (202) 857-0900—10 AM to 9 PM—7 Days a Week

Robert Guillaume as Nathan Detroit led his spiffily-dressed sharpsters in a grandstanding repentance before the skeptical sisters at the Save-A-Soul Mission in Guys and Dolls.

James Randolph was Sky Masterson, high-stakes gambler, and Ernestine Jackson was Sister Sarah Brown, his adversary-turned-sweetheart, in the highly successful black version of the ever-popular Guys and Dolls.

born at Washington's Arena Stage—came later.

Hallelujah, Baby! was a musical that charted the improving status of blacks in 20th Century America, arriving with popular singer Julius LaRosa in one of the few white roles. The *River Niger*, by Joseph A. Walker, was enthusiastically received, especially by the blacks who were in the majority at many performances, surely an unusual situation in the National's history. Thunderous shouts of "Right on, sister!" shook the house, and the evenings took on the electric zeal of a revival service as encouragement crackled both ways across the footlights. *What the Winesellers Buy* was another story of emerging black consciousness.

In 1977 came abrasively beautiful poetry in *For Colored Girls Who Have Considered Suicide/When The Rainbow Is Enuf.* That same year *Paul Robeson*, a biographical one-man show starring James Earl Jones, was a focus of contention. Pickets leafleted the opening night audience, complaining that the script stressed the tragic rather than the artistic and revolutionary aspects of Robeson's career. Paul Robeson, Jr. found the portrayal of his father "grossly distorted." City Councilman and later Mayor Marion Barry was "not so sure this play is as deep and serious as it should be."

New black audiences and greatly improved racial relations now encouraged producers to mount a succession of light-hearted (and too often light-headed) all-black plays and musicals in the 1970's and 80's. Among these were *Bubblin' Brown Sugar, One Mo' Time, Ain't Misbehavin', Daddy Goodness,* and *Purlie*, in addition to *It's Showdown Time*, "a black slam-bang downhome version of 'The Taming of the Shrew.' " Most of these shows were thinly plotted or plotless but they were gutsy, glitzy, and infectiously energetic. And most were enormously successful: they brought record numbers of Washington blacks and whites together to revel in Afro-American exuberance. The unrelenting emphasis on song-and-dance in these shows added little depth or dignity to the image of blacks, but brilliant vocal stylizations and splashy Harlem tap dancing won hearts of all stripes. When the shows arrived in "Chocolate City," as blacks cockily and whites sometimes derisively called the capital, the National Theatre rocked with rhythmic hand-clapping and unrestrained interracial joy.

Producers also tried revamping past hits in new all-black formats. Washington was targeted as a prime market for such shows. In 1979 the *chutzpah* of *Guys and Dolls* was replaced with soul-cool in a highly popular all-black revival featuring Robert Guillaume, later TV's "Benson." An attempt to move *Kismet* from Persia to *Timbuktu!* in a production featuring lynx-like Eartha Kitt was less successful. However, the sultry chanteuse—remembered in Washington for a White House luncheon contretemps with Lady Bird Johnson—was irrepressible as ever.

As *the* "Class-A Legitimate" theatre in Washington for much of the 20th Century, the National's attractions for the most part mirrored established trends and successes of Broadway show business. They reflected, too, the tastes of a conservative populace, in large part associated with the bureaus and agencies of the federal government. The National rarely staged the radical; therefore a few atypical attractions deserve mention.

In 1969 came *The Boys in the Band*, the first play centered primarily on homosexuality. Playwright Mart Crowley and director Bob Moore had both studied at Catholic University and a wag joked that their mentor, Father Hartke, knew the title of the show before he knew its content, and proudly proclaimed the advent of a "wonderful new musical" by his protégés.

Hair, the tradition-breaking musical of the "Age of Aquarius" came to the National in 1971. "Flower children" festooned the marquee with garlands of plastic daisies and laid grass carpeting from inner lobby to curbside. Special offices were set up next-door to the theatre in the Munsey building for the taking of reservations, as enormous lines formed at the box office. Orchestra seats were a hefty $10. (The following season subscribers were offered an orchestra seat *and* dinner at Bassin's restaurant for $12.50!). The entire scheduled 10-week run was sold out; in *Variety's* argot: a "750 G Advance." The show introduced frontal nudity—albeit swift and dimly lit—to the chaste National stage for the first time. Another innovation sent a rank of performers striding off the stage onto the armrests of the auditorium seating, stepping over the mink-hatted heads of matinee ladies who sat in stunned incredulity, or fled gasping to the Astro-Turfed exits. James Rado and Jerome Ragni, creators of the show's book and lyrics, were recent emigres from Washington. Rado had studied at Catholic University as James Radomski, and at Maryland University. Ragni, while serving in the army at Fort Myer, shed his combat boots on weekends and devised barefoot 'improvs' with hip local actors at Dupont Circle.

Hair remained 21 weeks at the National, after which the theatre closed for repairs. The now-grimy plastic daisies were removed, the offices next-door closed, and the wispy whiff of marijuana banished from the stairwells. The "laid-back" mien which had spread from stage to ushering staff was reversed: beads and bellbottoms were out, neckties were de rigueur.

THE NATIONAL BESIEGED

In 1950, after more than 50 years as a neighbor to the west, separated from the National only by the Munsey Building, the *Washington Post* moved from E Street up to L as the downtown began to decay. The handsome seven-story Romanesque-Revival *Post* building with its Indiana limestone facade was torn down not long after to make way for parking. The once-bustling Willard Hotel, in decline, finally closed its dusty doors. The

In Man of La Mancha, *Richard Kiley as Don Quixote and Tony Martinez as Sancho Panza rode dancing horses in quest of "The Impossible Dream." The musical returned year after year to the National with a succession of stars in the lead role.*

National, meanwhile, came for a time under management of The Nederlander Organization, family entrepreneurs soon to rank second only to the Shuberts in theatrical clout.

"National Theatre Nears End of an Extended Run," pronounced a *Washington Post* headline in 1963. Demolition of the National Theatre building and the adjacent Munsey was planned by Jerry Wollman, a Silver Spring builder, who bought the properties for $5 million and envisioned for the site a 13-story office building containing a mammoth new legitimate theatre. Architect Edmund Dreyfuss was engaged to design the structure and the playhouse, "twice the 1,683-seat capacity of the present National," with enlarged stage facilities to accommodate opera and ballet. The project,

Kiley's portrayal of the eccentric knight-errant was an incandescent tribute to heroism hidden in fumbling human nature.

123

Wollman hoped, would "fit into President Kennedy's ideas of a more handsome Pennsylvania Avenue." Fans of the National were apathetic, complained a writer to the *Post*, who lamented the "silence of the citizenry concerning this theatrical rape. . . . How loud and impassioned were the cries of Save the Shubert, Save the Belasco, and Save the Capitol. Doesn't anyone want to save the National?" The *Post did* want to, apparently, and editorialized against a larger theatre. Opera, thought the *Post*, would best be left to

> the future Cultural Center. The present National is, if anything too big. With its 1,683 seats, it is bigger than all but two of New York's 42 legitimate theatres. [It is] an indispensable enterprise which illuminates the whole life of the city.

Preservationists rose to protest the demolition of the Munsey building as well. Architect Dreyfuss had inadvertently reminded them that the structure was designed early in the century by the internationally famous architect, Stanford White. White was infamous as well, having been gunned down at the opening of the old Madison Square Garden in New York by millionaire Harry K. Thaw, who accused the architect of "ruining" his wife, the celebrated beauty and "showgirl," Evelyn Nesbit.

Wollman, chastened by the aesthetic uproar, announced that he was a Washingtonian and "could not be more concerned over the city's cultural assets, of which the National is the most prominent." That ended this proposal to demolish the buildings.

Nevertheless, by the 1970s the National had fallen on hard times. Downtown Washington was urban-blighted, the splendid new John F. Kennedy Center for the Performing Arts had lured away mugger-shy patrons, and tickets went unsold. The Nederlander Organization was losing money and wanted to bail out. Jimmy Nederlander brought the matter up with his longtime friend Roger L. Stevens, Chairman of the Kennedy Center. Would the Center be interested, Nederlander wondered, in taking over the lease to keep the National alive? A non-profit organization, he mused, might succeed where a commercial corporation could not.

Stevens thought the idea a capital one, but outside the mandate of the Center. Therefore, at the end of 1974, he and others formed the non-profit New National Theatre Corporation to take over the affairs of the theatre. Maurice Tobin, a dynamic young lawyer, became president of the new board, which included

Bobbysox, leather jackets, duck-tail haircuts, and poodle skirts flourished at Rydell High in numerous return engagements of the indestructible musical, Grease. *A flame-emblazoned hot rod, hard-driving rhythms, teenage sass, and youthful innocence were among the show's enduring attractions.*

his wife, Joan Fleischmann Tobin; arts patrons Aldus Chapin and Gerson Nordlinger, Jr.; impresario Patrick Hayes; Georgetown University theatre professor Donn B. Murphy, Ph.D.; and Jack Ryan, President of the Stagehands' Union.

The new board contracted with The Kennedy Center for booking and management services. Attractions were scheduled, and it appeared that a national cultural treasure had been saved as the theatre passed from 139 years of commercial operation to the control of a non-profit board.

Scott Kirkpatrick had been succeeded by his assistant, Ted Luck, who soon withdrew from the hurly-burly of theatrical management to become a school teacher. He was followed by Richard E. "Rick" Schneider, who had managed the Eisenhower Theater and had been a company manager in New York. Schneider, unlike his predecessors, was more the business manager and technician than the greeter. As it turned out, the theatre was dark during much of his tenure, and he prowled by flashlight through basements and attics, noting with camera and tape-measure the cracks which were creeping across the plaster, and more worrisome fissures snaking across the auditorium floor and the concrete foundations of the deteriorating building. He also established an archive and began the retrieval of the National's long-scattered memorabilia.

The first production under the new management, *All Over Town*, directed by Dustin Hoffman, received a mixed reception. With *Bubblin' Brown Sugar* the National had a summertime hit, but financial losses followed on succeeding shows. A surefire star booking was on the way, however: Katharine Hepburn was announced in a comedy for the fall of 1975. On the morning Hepburn arrived, she cast a baleful eye at the auditorium. Paint was peeling, and just above the east wall boxes was a patch of crumbling plaster. The actress explained sweetly but firmly to the manager that if *he* did not repair the wall, *she would*. Knowing that a hot audience is an inattentive one, the New England-bred Hepburn also suggested politely that the air-conditioning *would* be turned *on* for the November run. Her requests accommodated, the star returned the favor and delighted the city at sellout performances of *A Matter of Gravity*.

Still, at the end of its first year, the New National Theatre Board was becoming restive over the quality and number of bookings. While The Kennedy Center stages seemed constantly surfeited with interesting fare, The National often languished. By spring, however, there was excitement again with a season of attractions scheduled, including the popular comedy, *Same Time Next Year*, the prestigious drama *Equus*, and the durable musical, *Grease*.

Now the theatre was long overdue for renovation. Scarlet seats were installed on the old cast-iron standards, while walls and ceiling of the auditorium were painted cream-of-tomato red. The existing soft yellow house curtain remained, as did draperies of the same satin in alcoves behind the boxes. The now-venerable white eagle and thirteen stars above the proscenium were gilded. Colonial wall-sconces, each with five electric candles, brightened the auditorium, and brass fixtures replaced glass chandeliers in the stairwells and lobbies. Worn wallscaping was removed, and acoustic panels applied to the balcony walls. Lobbies were painted ivory and carpeted in red.

The stage floor had deteriorated over the years from the incision of countless trapdoors. Jerrybuilt supports in the basement threatened collapse. Technicians for *Annie*, the musical slated to reopen the house, warned that the weary floor would send the show's heavy deck with its several treadmills crashing into the cellar. A new floor made up of modular sections was installed on removable steel beams and columns, creating great flexibility for future productions.

The nation's official portrait of Helen Hayes, by Furman Finck, on loan from The National Portrait Gallery, was hung in the second floor lobby. Miss Hayes, "First Lady of the American Theatre," came for the official unveiling. Standing on the stage she had commanded so often and casting her eyes up to the far reaches of "the gods," she recalled that she saw her first play "right here at the National." When it was over, she remembered, she clung to her chair high in the balcony and refused to leave, hoping that the actors would reappear and "start all over . . . I didn't want to leave the theatre—and I guess I really never have."

The refurbished playhouse had barely reopened when it came under threat of extinction once again, this time from the forces of downtown renewal. President Kennedy, surveying the inelegance of Pennsylvania Avenue as he passed along the nation's rundown ceremonial avenue on his Inaugural Day almost twenty years before, had determined to rejuvenate the nation's "main street." Events he set in motion resulted in the creation of the Pennsylvania Avenue Development Corporation, known in acronym-loving Washington as "PADC." Given the power of eminent domain, PADC could condemn old buildings along Pennsylvania Avenue, raze them, and assemble attractive "packages" for renewal by interested developers. Once a parcel of land was assembled, PADC wrote a prospectus extolling the potential of the property in question. Circulated to developers, the prospectus solicited imaginative development proposals.

PADC chose as one of its first challenges renewal of the block on which the theatre sits. Forthwith it condemned and purchased most of the properties bounded by E and F Streets, and 13th and 14th Streets. These were combined into a single parcel for long-term lease. Plans for a competition to select a developer for the site were well underway before the New National Theatre Board became aware of what was afoot. PADC

An actress and a president exchanged greetings backstage after Liv Ullmann performed Eugene O'Neill's Anna Christie *for an enthusiastic audience including President Jimmy Carter.*

asked developers to include some sort of performance space in their projects but did not require saving of the National Theatre building. The suddenly alarmed board tried vainly to persuade PADC that preserving the theatre should be a condition of the award, but PADC countered that it could not show favoritism, even to the oldest cultural institution in the city. Thus the very existence of the National Theatre was once again at jeopardy. Lowe's Palace Theatre on F Street was quickly demolished, as were the old Blue Mirror and Ceres restaurants, where so many theatre patrons had lunched before the matinee, or supped following the evening performance. Soon little remained on the block other

Robert Donley and Liv Ullmann brought power and pathos to Eugene O'Neill's script, but one line prompted unanticipated laughter: The audience, knowing that President Carter was a peanut farmer, were amused when Anna's father was asked if he "would have Anna lying down at night with a muddy scut, stinking of pigs and peanuts and dung."

IN LINE FOR THE BIG BREAK

When *A Chorus Line*, one of the all-time great successes of the American theatre, played Washington, life imitated art: Local dancers were invited to try out for roles in a musical that was all about auditioning for a Broadway play. The exhilaration and heartbreak of theatrical competition was evident on the National stage and also in the lobbies as hopeful hoofers tried to get in step for their big break.

The Broadway company portrays the tension of a dance audition.

A Washington dancer makes his bid for fame.

Washington's aspiring auditionees experience the reality of trying out on the National stage.

A spangled apotheosis for winners was the finale of A Chorus Line. This psychodramatic contest, in which Broadway beginners bare their souls, mesmerized audiences with arresting revelations and unvarnished honesty.

than the National Press Club, the doomed Munsey building, and the National Theatre.

The parcel was certainly an attractive prize. Across Pennsylvania Avenue was the District Building, Washington's "City Hall." At 14th Street stood the magnificent old Willard Hotel, derelict, but slated for glorious rehabilitation. The National found itself endangered, but courted by developers seeking to make a match with the theatre. Some developers began to feel that PADC might look favorably on a plan which retained the building, particularly since the National Board was becoming increasingly vocal on the issue and was successfully recruiting powerful support. Impassioned curtain-call speeches were being made nightly by Carol Channing, who cast her arms wide and implored, "Don't let them destroy this lovely old playhouse! Rome saved its Colosseum. We've got to save our National Theatre!" The board's choice among developers was perilous indeed: All made alluring overtures, but to select the wrong one could prove disastrous.

John Portman, the celebrated Atlanta architect who pioneered the dazzling atrium hotel now imitated worldwide, wanted to raze the theatre. In partnership with the National Press Club, he proposed to build new quarters for the club, a 1,000-room hotel with an atrium "the size of two football fields" and a 700-seat theatre. National Theatre representatives explained that so few seats would be a poor exchange for the National's 1,683, and would not prove economically viable for professional touring shows. Portman offered a 1,000-seat theatre and then a 1,400-seat subterranean playhouse at 14th and F Streets. Roger Stevens pronounced these unacceptable, and the New National Theatre Board agreed.

Portman then wondered if the National might move operations to the Warner Theatre, a 2,000-seat presentation house nearby on 14th Street boasting a marble staircase and far more ornate plasterwork than the sedate National. When the Board remained unmoved, Portman and the Press Club advanced a final grand scheme for a new freestanding theatre to be built on 13th Street between E Street and Pennsylvania Avenue, if that site could be somehow secured and funds for the theatre collected. Portman's visionary rendering showed a dramatic "cylindrical auditorium set in a glass cube outer wall, the lobby surrounding the theatre at the full height of the auditorium." The theatre would be fresh, new, and have a commanding seat on the ceremonial avenue. Cognizant of the existing National's shabby dressing rooms, crowded lobbies, and embarrassingly archaic lavatories, board members looked covetously at Portman's awesome crystalline show-

The American premiere engagement of the distinguished Amadeus *brought to the National stage a coquettish Jane Seymour as the wife of Mozart, and Ian McKellan as the envious antagonist,* Court Composer Salieri.

case. Still, nostalgic affection for the old building remained, as did determination not to dislodge an institution from the ground it had held for more than 140 years. In any case there was no assurance that land or money for a new structure was available. Washingtonians, many of whom—like Helen Hayes—had seen their first live theatre at the National, were not likely to underwrite the dreams of a board which had conspired in the demolition of their beloved playhouse.

Presently Robert Gladstone of Quadrangle Development Corporation appeared on the scene with plans for a flagship Marriott hotel, a shopping arcade, and an office building. Gladstone pledged to retain the National Theatre building and suggested that additional space could be made available to expand the theatre's stingy lounges and cramped dressing rooms. John Akridge, another local developer, also submitted a plan which allowed for saving the theatre.

The National Board met with the several developers, seeking promise of specific improvements in exchange for endorsement of their proposals. Prior to the all-

The Odd Couple, in Neil Simon's gender-switching reincarnation, came for a tryout with Rita Moreno, who had starred previously at the National, and Sally Struthers, essaying her first Broadway part after a long run in the highly successful series All In The Family *on television.*

important meeting at which PADC would vote on one of the three development options, the National publicly rejected the Portman proposal and endorsed the other two. The choice was now up to PADC, and in 1978 the right to develop the site, with a mandate to rehabilitate the National, went to Quadrangle/Marriott and their investment partners. There followed a four-year negotiation among representatives of Quadrangle/Marriott, PADC, and the National, as several general agreements were hammered into thousands of specific lease terms and blueprint details.

Meanwhile, all was not well with the National's Kennedy Center management arrangement. The Board sensed increasingly that the National was too frequently playing second-string to the Center. Hit musicals came to the National only on return swings through Washington, following prestigious first-run engagements at the Center. Bookings seemed sparse and the National was again perceived as an unexciting auxiliary to the main attraction in town. A constant irritant was

Two suave Latin lovers, in the persons of Tony Shalhoub and Lewis J. Stadlen, court the bachelorettes, one diffident, one delighted, in a hilarious scene of linguistic and amorous misconstructions.

From 1862 to 1873 the National sported a balcony just above the theatre entrance. A group of gentlemen, including theatre manager William W. Rapley and perhaps also habitués of Deery's Billiard Saloon located on the second floor of the theatre building, pose there in 1868.

Facing Pennsylvania Avenue from the same location for 150 years, although frequently rebuilt and redecorated, the National Theatre has served every generation of Washingtonians since 1835. Enduring stiff competition at times, the National was at other periods the only Washington theatre where live performances could be seen. Throughout many changes of commercial management, and now as a nonprofit theatre, Washington's most cherished playhouse has always mirrored the fashions and foibles of the times.

The New National Theatre which opened in 1885 boasted a twin-towered street front in Italianate style. The acoustics of the house were considered nearly perfect, and the five-storied building remained basically unaltered until 1922.

The design that saved the National, shown here almost as it looked when completed in 1984, joined the theatre to a hotel-and-office complex which includes an arcade of 140 shops. The theatre facade remained unchanged except at street level, where floor-to-ceiling windows look out from the enlarged lobby, and a re-designed marquee mimics the old one shown in this sketch.

An unrealized scheme for the site proposed a sleek hotel and a modern treatment for the theatre (suggested at right in the model). On Western Plaza (not then built) are two controversial pylons which were never approved.

CHANGING PROGRAMS

Heroic women, a naked nymph, and svelte carriage-trade patrons are among the fanciful figures which have adorned the National Theatre's playbill covers. Architectural motifs and the ever-popular masks of comedy and tragedy have also graced the programs. The name of the playbill and of the theatre itself have varied as fashions changed. Under Kennedy Center management during a period in the 1970s, the National Theatre's program covers suffered the odd indignity of displaying only photos of the Kennedy Center.

1906

1908

1911

1915

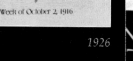

1916

1926

1932

1933

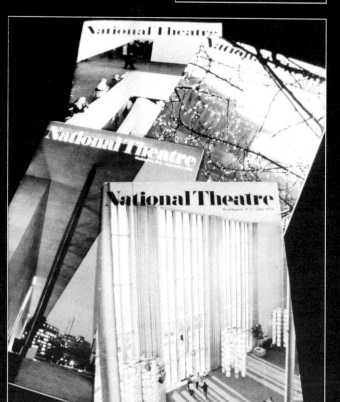

the National's playbill, supplied by the publisher of the Kennedy Center programs, and emblazoned each month with a color photo of the Center—graphically certifying the secondary status of the National.

In a bold move, National Theatre President Tobin led the board in a declaration of independence from the Kennedy Center in 1979. The Nederlander Organization wished to regain the theatre it had jettisoned, and other Broadway producers made management proposals to the board. Backed by the enormous booking power and financial stability of the highly regarded Shubert Organization, Gerald Schoenfeld and Bernard Jacobs finally won the confidence of the National Board.

The National Theatre building, however, was far from stable, due to massive excavations beginning on the block. The structures to the east of the theatre had been razed to make way for a new office building, and to the west the Munsey building was demolished. As these structures which had buttressed the soil surrounding the National disappeared, fears for the safety of the theatre arose. Tiber Creek still flows deep beneath Washington and the theatre's ancient footings stand on a pad of wet clay thirty to forty feet deep. Unsupported on either side, and with the water table falling, the theatre's foundations began to move. Plaster fell from the auditorium ceilings, doors began to stick, and the weary steam-heat system started to leak. Concerned contractors thrust a slurry wall deep into the earth on the theatre's north and west sides to stabilize the water table. An underpinning of steel caissons was driven beneath the National's old foundations, as a squadron of engineers arrived to monitor alarming fissures in the old theatre's walls.

Increasingly frustrated with the sluggish renovation negotiations and the deteriorating theatre, and disagreeing with the Shubert Organization over management procedures, President Tobin threatened to shut down the theatre. It did close in the spring of 1982 for what became an 18-month renovation period. A new heating and air-conditioning system was installed throughout, and a new five-story backstage building was constructed with spacious and well-lighted dressing rooms, a small rehearsal hall, a wardrobe shop, and a place for the theatre Archive. At the entrance to the theatre, spaces formerly occupied by a barber shop to the west and a jewelry store and the Curtain Call cafe to the east were captured to allow expansion of the first floor lobby to three times its previous size. On the second-level terrazzo mezzanine, the offices of the theatre manager and the New National Theatre Corporation were removed in order to triple the public space and create the new Helen Hayes Gallery. A mini-stage was installed at the east end of this room to accommodate the free programming which had begun to attract appreciative if uncomfortably crowded community audiences on Saturday mornings. The theatre management offices were moved to a suite on the third

Under its new nonprofit charter, the National Theatre board began in the 1970s a number of free programs which forged new links between the theatre and the community. George C. Scott spoke at a noontime forum.

floor, and the non-profit corporation offices were located in new space acquired on the fourth floor. Elevators were installed backstage for the actors, and at the front of the house for patrons.

Manager Rick Schneider left to pursue law studies, and Harry Teter, Jr., an attorney, stock theatre producer, and former president of the New National Theatre Corporation, became General Manager. Virginia businessman John B. Adams, Jr. succeeded Maurice Tobin as Chairman, and Donn Murphy became President.

The developer's renovation—first estimated at $3,000,000, and eventually costing $6,000,000—had never been expected to include re-carpeting the auditorium, renewing light fixtures, and replacing upholstery and draperies. This interior work was accomplished on an interest-free $1.5 million loan from the Shubert Organization, to be paid back from box office income. Adding luxury touches to the basic Quadrangle/Marriott renovation, "the Shuberts," as the firm continues to be dubbed years after the departure of the famous founders, were able to create one of the finest theatres in America. Stage wiring was overhauled, 137

Three break-dancers crackle and pop on Western Plaza in front of the theatre. This SATURDAY MORNING AT THE NATIONAL event drew a record-breaking crowd of 15,000 people, many of them fans cheering on a dozen teams which competed in vigorous gymnastic dance.

backstage cueing systems improved, and the latest computer ticketing system installed in the new box office.

Oliver Smith was brought aboard to supervise the elaborate interior decoration. Smith, whose settings for many productions, including *My Fair Lady* and *West Side Story*, had been seen in this house, was now designing his first theatre. He effected a return to the Georgian Regency motif suggested in the theatre's architecture by making the auditorium walls and stairwells a "sharp robin's egg blue," and setting against this a Prussian blue carpet. Seats were covered in light melon velvet, and a variant of this color used on the walls of the second-level Helen Hayes Gallery. The arresting color combination, Smith explained, was contemporary but also very traditional: In country manors and town houses designed by Scottish architect Robert

Adam in the 18th Century, just such vibrant colors had been used to brighten the long gray English winters.

Long-obscured details in the theatre's ceiling were highlighted with gilt, and additional plasterwork was added to the proscenium, boxes, and lobbies. Two great crystal chandeliers were designed for the auditorium, which heretofore had none. A stage curtain woven in a peach tone harmonious with the seats was hung, and the same fabric used for the mini-stage in the Helen Hayes Gallery. The Italian government, and marble quarries, presented the theatre with panels of Sicilian perlatto for the main lobby, and the Ambassador of Saudi Arabia underwrote its installation.

THE NATIONAL TRIUMPHANT

Having survived several seasons and many storms, the weathered nonprofit board dropped the "new" from its name and became the National Theatre Corporation. At last the National Theatre seemed secure, with a 99-year property lease, $7,500,000 worth of plant improvements, and a management agreement with the Shubert

At a free performance, outreach director Kathleen Barry introduced native Washingtonian and Broadway star Brooke Johns, who sang again on the National stage, where he had starred with W.C. Fields in the Ziegfeld Follies some 60 years earlier.

Organization, indisputably the most eminent theatrical producers in America. There seemed little doubt, presuming that good shows were available for touring, that the house would continue to serve as a Washington showplace for the best available class-A legitimate touring attractions for many years to come.

In addition, the theatre had established a number of free public service activities. *Saturday Morning at the National*, a free children's program, continued with support from the neighboring J.W. Marriott Hotel. Performances were held in the Helen Hayes Gallery, where so many Broadway-bound shows had rehearsed. Clowns, storytellers and musicians appeared week by week, and Washington's cultural diversity was reflected as flamenco dancers, African drummers, German folk musicians, and Irish step-dancers performed. Blacks, whites, Hispanics, and Orientals in combined groups participated when the theatre sponsored a breakdance competition in 1984. The contest drew 15,000 persons to Western Plaza, directly in front of the National, the largest audience ever assembled on the capital's town square up to that time.

Free programs each Monday evening in the Helen

Hayes Gallery showcased local actors, new playscripts, opera excerpts, poetry, comedians, and tap dancers. A Summer Cinema Series began. Services for the disabled were established, including infrared amplification through headsets, and scheduled signed performances for the hearing-impaired. The National began providing the vision-impaired with narrations of the mainstage performances, and has the first broadcast booth for this purpose ever installed in a theatre.

In cooperation with the Shubert Organization, a Special Patron Ticket Program was established with half-price tickets for students and senior citizens. The National Theatre Corporation created an Endowed Ticket Fund to sponsor free admission for groups of children, including Washington students with perfect school attendance records, the offspring of parents killed in service to their country, and youngsters with terminal illnesses.

And so, in January of 1984, arc lights swept the night sky and a gala reopening marked the rebirth of a dramatically renewed playhouse. Onstage was *42nd Street*, a musical extravaganza based on the 1933 motion picture classic. The tale of theatrical heartbreak and ulti-

Liv Ullmann was surrounded by a group of admiring Brownies after a Saturday morning appearance in which she held a large audience of children spellbound. Just back from a tour of famine-ravaged lands, the actress encouraged the Brownies to be aware of the problem of hungry children around the world. In its 150th year, the National remains as young as its audience.

mate success was poignantly appropriate for the occasion. Helen Hayes made a toast, and an afterpiece was spoken from the stage by President Ronald Reagan, who had watched the performance from the front box at the east side of the auditorium. Introducing himself and Mrs. Reagan as the National's "neighbors," the Chief Executive marvelled at the longevity of the historic theatre. Indeed, the National had outlived even the street on which it stood, for the audience filed out onto a block of the former E Street, recently rechristened "Pennsylvania Avenue North."

On December 7, 1985, the National Theatre marked the 150th anniversary of its founding, and friends recalled its rich past. From fire and failure the phoenix had repeatedly risen to triumph. The next act in the colorful cavalcade of this "Theatre of the Presidents" remains to be played, but the spangled panoply of its first 150 years stands as a veritable history of the American theatre. And the long survival of the National Theatre itself is a drama as stirring and grand as any yet acted on this remarkable stage for a nation.

CURTAIN

ACKNOWLEDGEMENTS

The National Theatre wishes to express its gratitude to the Gould Foundation for its initiative and financial support which made the production of this book possible.

Our thanks and appreciation to the following for their generous assistance: Kathleen Barry, Jimmie Been, Bill Bennett, Robert Boyer, Elsie Carper, Jon Carrow, Ed Cashman, Ellie Chamberlain, Richard L. Coe, Steven Crowley, Patrick Ford, Martin Gottfried, Lucy Gregory, Austin Hay, Patrick Hayes, Julia Heflin, Richard Kidwell, Bob Lawrence, Joe Lewis, Martha R. Mahard, Adolphe Meyer, Elizabeth Miller, Stephen Moore, Ed Platt, Hank Reynolds, Rick Schneider, Tom Shorebird, Leo Sullivan, Dorothy L. Swerdlove, Fred Tepper, Alma Viator, the staffs of the Columbia Historical Society, the Washingtonia Collection at the Martin Luther King Library, and the Performing Arts Library, a joint project of the Library of Congress and the John F. Kennedy Center for the Performing Arts, and the National Geographic Society.

ILLUSTRATION CREDITS

The sources for the illustrations in this book are shown below.

COVER Joseph H. Bailey. Back cover inset—The National Theatre. Inside-upper, David Alan Harvey; lower, Joseph H. Bailey. Front and back end papers—The National Theatre.

7—National Portrait Gallery, Smithsonian Institution, Washington, D.C. 8 upper and lower left—Joseph H. Bailey, The National Theatre. 8 lower right— Library of Congress. 9 left—Harvard Theatre Collection. 9 right—Joseph H. Bailey. 10,11—Joseph H. Bailey. 12,13—Martha Swope Associates/Carol Rosegg. 12 lower—Joan Marcus, The National Theatre.

CHAPTER ONE 14,16,17,18—Library of Congress. 19—Theatre Arts Library, Harry Ransom Humanities Research Center, The University of Texas at Austin. 20 left—Library of Congress. 20 right—*The National Intelligencer*, D.C. Public Library. 21 left—Harvard Theatre Collection. 21 right—*The National Intelligencer*, D.C. Public Library. 22—Harvard Theatre Collection. 23,24,25,26—Library of Congress. 27 left—from *Domestic Manners of the Americans*, by Frances Trollope. 27 right—*The National Intelligencer*, D.C. Public Library. 28,29—Library of Congress. 30,31—Joseph H. Bailey, *Perley's Reminiscences of Sixty Years In The National Metropolis*, 1886. 32—Library of Congress. 35—Harvard Theatre Collection. 36,37,39,40—Library of Congress.

CHAPTER TWO 42—Library of Congress. 44—Theatre Arts Library, Harry Ransom Humanities Research Center, The University of Texas at Austin. 45—Joseph H. Bailey, The National Theatre. 46,47—Library of Congress. 48,49—Billy Rose Theatre Collection; The New York Public Library at Lincoln Center; Astor, Lenox and Tilden Foundations. 50—Library of Congress. 51,52—Harvard Theatre Collection. 54 upper, 55—Library of Congress. 54 lower, 56 left—Joseph H. Bailey, D.C. Public Library. 57 upper, 58 upper—Billy Rose Theatre Collection; The New York Public Library at Lincoln Center; Astor, Lenox and Tilden Foundations. 58 lower, 59—Joseph H. Bailey, The National Theatre. 60—Billy Rose Theatre Collection; The New York Public Library at Lincoln Center; Astor, Lenox and Tilden Foundations. 61—Joseph H. Bailey, The National Theatre. 62 upper—Joseph H. Bailey, D.C. Public Library. 62 lower, 64 lower—Library of Congress. 64 upper, 65—Culver Pictures. 66,67—Library of Congress. 68,69,70,71,72,73 lower—Billy Rose Theatre Collection; The New York Public Library at Lincoln Center; Astor, Lenox and Tilden Foundations. 73 upper—Culver Pictures. 74 upper—AP/Wide World Photos. 74 lower—Underwood & Underwood. 75—Billy Rose Theatre Collection; The New York Public Library at Lincoln Center; Astor, Lenox and Tilden Foundations. 76,77,79—© *The Washington Post*.

81—Library of Congress. 82 upper—Gjon Mili, LIFE Magazine © 1957 Time Inc. 82 lower left—John Dominis, LIFE Magazine © 1962 Time Inc. 82 lower right—Mark Kauffman, LIFE Magazine © 1967 Time Inc. 83—Hank Walker, LIFE Magazine © 1957 Time Inc. 84 upper—Robert Knudsen, The Lyndon Baines Johnson Library. 84 middle—John Dominis, LIFE Magazine © 1967 Time Inc. 84 lower left—Mark Kauffman, LIFE Magazine © 1964 Time Inc. 84,85,86,87,88—Martha Swope.

CHAPTER THREE 90—George Tames/NYT PICTURES. 92—Billy Rose Theatre Collection; The New York Public Library at Lincoln Center; Astor, Lenox and Tilden Foundations. 93 left—Joseph H. Bailey, The National Theatre. 93 upper right—Philippe Halsman, LIFE Magazine © 1949 Time Inc. 94 left—Culver Pictures. 94 right, 95—Billy Rose Theatre Collection; The New York Public Library at Lincoln Center; Astor, Lenox and Tilden Foundations. 96 left—Joseph H. Bailey, The National Theatre. 96 right, 97—The National Theatre. 99—Billy Rose Theatre Collection; The New York Public Library at Lincoln Center; Astor, Lenox and Tilden Foundations. 100—D.C. Public Library. 101 upper—Joseph H. Bailey, © *The Washington Post*. Reprinted by permission of the D.C. Public Library. 101 middle—Joseph H. Bailey, D.C. Public Library. 102— Joseph H. Bailey, The National Theatre. 103—The National Theatre. 104,105—John F. Kennedy Library. 105 right—Joseph H. Bailey, The National Theatre. 106—Joseph H. Bailey, © *The Washington Post*. Reprinted by permission of the D.C. Public Library. 107 upper—Joseph H. Bailey, © *The Washington Post*. Reprinted by permission of the D.C. Public Library. 107 lower—Billy Rose The-

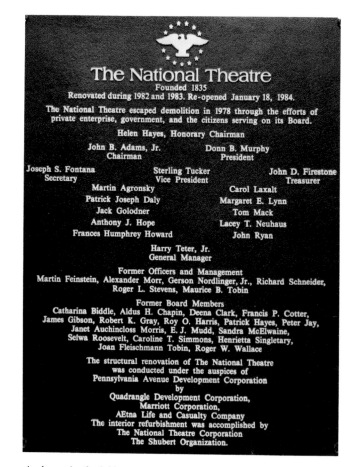

The National Theatre

Founded 1835
Renovated during 1982 and 1983. Re-opened January 18, 1984.

The National Theatre escaped demolition in 1978 through the efforts of private enterprise, government, and the citizens serving on its Board.

Helen Hayes, Honorary Chairman

John B. Adams, Jr.
Chairman

Donn B. Murphy
President

Joseph S. Fontana
Secretary

Sterling Tucker
Vice President

John D. Firestone
Treasurer

Martin Agronsky

Patrick Joseph Daly

Jack Golodner

Anthony J. Hope

Frances Humphrey Howard

Carol Laxalt

Margaret E. Lynn

Tom Mack

Lacey T. Neuhaus

John Ryan

Harry Teter, Jr.
General Manager

Former Officers and Management
Martin Feinstein, Alexander Morr, Gerson Nordlinger, Jr., Richard Schneider,
Roger L. Stevens, Maurice B. Tobin

Former Board Members
Catharina Biddle, Aldus H. Chapin, Deena Clark, Francis P. Cotter,
James Gibson, Robert K. Gray, Roy O. Harris, Patrick Hayes, Peter Jay,
Janet Auchincloss Morris, E. J. Mudd, Sandra McElwaine,
Selwa Roosevelt, Caroline T. Simmons, Henrietta Singletary,
Joan Fleischmann Tobin, Roger W. Wallace

The structural renovation of The National Theatre
was conducted under the auspices of
Pennsylvania Avenue Development Corporation
by
Quadrangle Development Corporation,
Marriott Corporation,
AEtna Life and Casualty Company
The interior refurbishment was accomplished by
The National Theatre Corporation
The Shubert Organization.

A plaque in the lobby commemorates the reopening of the National in 1984 after its most recent renovation. In the list of board members and theatre administrators who saved the theatre from destruction and restored it are names prominent in Washington and beyond.

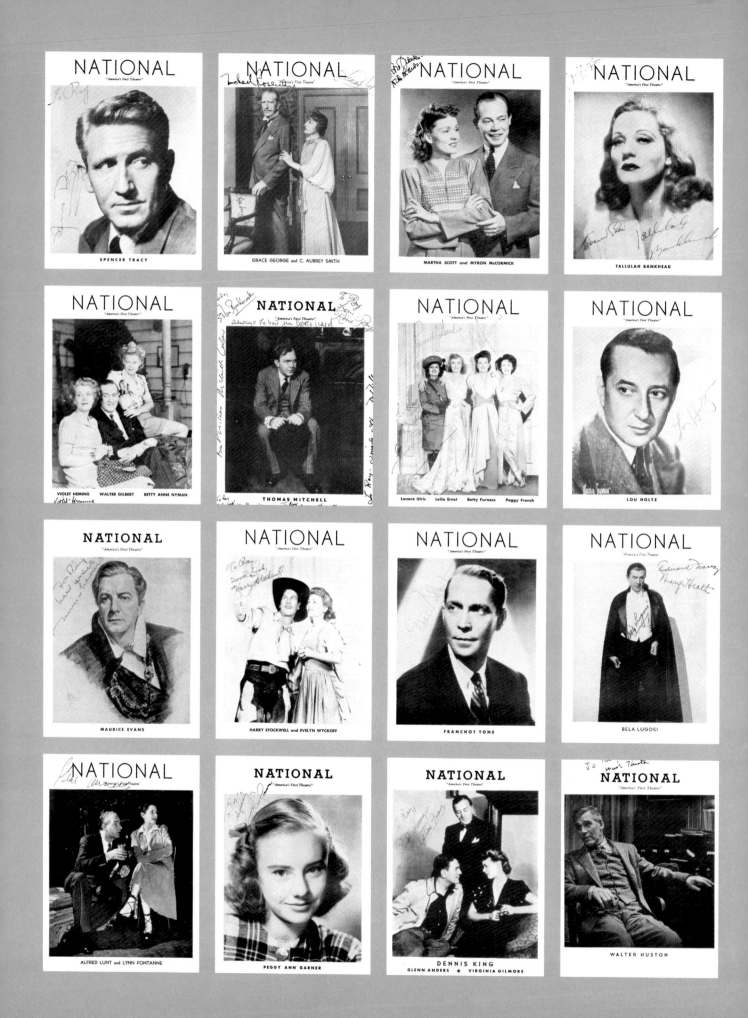

NATIONAL

SPENCER TRACY

GRACE GEORGE and C. AUBREY SMITH

MARTHA SCOTT and MYRON McCORMICK

TALLULAH BANKHEAD

VIOLET HEMING   WALTER GILBERT   BETTY ANNE NYMAN

THOMAS MITCHELL

Lenore Ulric   Leila Ernst   Betty Furness   Peggy French

LOU HOLTZ

MAURICE EVANS

HARRY STOCKWELL and EVELYN WYCKOFF

FRANCHOT TONE

BELA LUGOSI

ALFRED LUNT and LYNN FONTANNE

PEGGY ANN GARNER

DENNIS KING
GLENN ANDERS   ★   VIRGINIA GILMORE

WALTER HUSTON